SHAKESPEARE

TWELFTH NIGHT

NOTES

COLES EDITORIAL BOARD

Bound to stay open

Publisher's Note

Otabind (Ota-bind). This book has been bound using the patented Otabind process. You can open this book at any page, gently run your finger down the spine, and the pages will lie flat.

ABOUT COLES NOTES

COLES NOTES have been an indispensible aid to students on five continents since 1948.

COLES NOTES are available for a wide range of individual literary works. Clear, concise explanations and insights are provided along with interesting interpretations and evaluations.

Proper use of COLES NOTES will allow the student to pay greater attention to lectures and spend less time taking notes. This will result in a broader understanding of the work being studied and will free the student for increased participation in discussions.

COLES NOTES are an invaluable aid for review and exam preparation as well as an invitation to explore different interpretive paths.

COLES NOTES are written by experts in their fields. It should be noted that any literary judgement expressed herein is just that — the judgement of one school of thought. Interpretations that diverge from, or totally disagree with any criticism may be equally valid.

COLES NOTES are designed to supplement the text and are not intended as a substitute for reading the text itself. Use of the NOTES will serve not only to clarify the work being studied, but should enhance the reader's enjoyment of the topic.

ISBN 0-7740-3236-7

© COPYRIGHT 1996 AND PUBLISHED BY
COLES PUBLISHING COMPANY
TORONTO—CANADA
PRINTED IN CANADA

Manufactured by Webcom Limited
Cover finish: Webcom's Exclusive **Duracoat**

CONTENTS

WILLIAM SHAKESPEARE LIFE AND WORKS

Biographical Sketch

With the epithet "Dear Son of Memory", Milton praised Shakespeare as one constantly in our memories and brother of the Muses. Certainly no other author has held such sway over the literary world, undiminished through some three and a half centuries of shifting artistic tastes. Shakespeare's plots and his characters have continued to be a living reality for us; as his well known contemporary Ben Jonson wrote, in a familiar tribute, "Thou . . . art alive still, while thy Booke doth live,/ And we have wits to read, and praise to give."

The Early Years

Despite such acclaim and the scholarship it has spawned, our knowledge of Shakespeare's life is sketchy, filled with more questions than answers, even after we prune away the misinformation accumulated over the years. He was baptized on April 26, 1564, in Holy Trinity Church, Stratford-on-Avon. As it was customary to baptize children a few days after birth, we conjecture that he was born on April 23. The monument erected in Stratford states that he died on April 23, 1616, in his fifty-third year.

William was the third child of John Shakespeare, who came to Stratford from Snitterfield before 1532 as a "whyttawer" (tanner) and glover, and Mary Arden, daughter of a wealthy "gentleman of worship" from Wilmecote. They married around 1557. Since John Shakespeare owned one house on Greenhill Street and two on Henley Street, we cannot be certain where William was born, though the Henley Street shrine draws many tourists each year. William's two older sisters died in infancy, but three brothers and two other sisters survived at least into childhood.

Shakespeare's father was fairly well-to-do, dealing in farm products and wool, and owning considerable property in Stratford. After holding a series of minor municipal offices he was elected alderman in 1565, high bailiff (roughly similar to the mayor of today) in 1568, and chief alderman in 1571. There are no records of young Will Shakespeare's education (though there are many unfounded legends), but he undoubtedly attended the town school maintained by the burgesses, which prepared its students for the universities. Ben Jonson's line about Shakespeare's having "small *Latine*, and lesse *Greeke*" refers not to his education but to his lack of indebtedness to the classical writers and dramatists.

On November 27, 1582, a licence to marry was issued to "Willelmum Shaxpere *et* Annam Whateley *de* Temple Grafton," and on the next day a marriage bond for "Willm Shagspere" and "Anne Hathwey of Stratford" was signed by Fulk Sandells and John Richardson, farmers of Stratford. This bond stated that there was no "lawful let or impediment by reason of any precontract, consanguinity, affinity, or by any other lawful means whatsoever"; thus "William and Anne (were) to be married together with once asking of the banns of matrimony." The problem of Anne Whateley has led many researchers and some detractors to argue all kinds of improbabilities, such as the existence of two different Shakespeares and the forging of documents to conceal Shakespeare's true identity. The actual explanation seems to be simple: the clerk who made the marriage licence entry apparently copied the name "Whateley" from a preceding entry, as a glance at the full sheet suggests. (Incidentally, Nicholas Rowe in his life of Shakespeare, published in 1709, well before the discovery of these marriage records, gave Anne's name as Hathaway.) The problems of marriage with Anne Hathaway — he was eighteen and she was twenty-six — and of the bond have caused similar consternation. Why did these two marry when there was such a discrepancy of age? Why only one saying of the banns (rather than the usual three)? Why the emphasis on a possible legal impediment? The answer here is not simple or definite, but the birth of a daughter Susanna, baptized at Holy Trinity on May 26, 1583, seems to explain the odd circumstances. It should be recognized, however, that an engagement to marry was considered legally binding in those days (we still have breach-of-promise suits today) and that premarital relations were not unusual or frowned upon when an engagement had taken place. The circumstances already mentioned, Shakespeare's ensuing activities, and his will bequeathing to Anne "my second best bed with the furniture" have suggested to some that their marriage was not entirely happy. Their other children, the twins Hamnet and Judith, were christened on February 2, 1585.

Theatrical Life

Shakespeare's years before and immediately after the time of his marriage are not charted, but rumor has him as an apprentice to a master butcher or as a country teacher or an actor with some provincial company. He is supposed to have run away from whatever he was doing for livelihood and to have gone to London, where he soon attached himself to some theatrical group. At this time there were only two professional houses established in the London environs, The Theatre (opened in 1576) and The Curtain (opened in 1577). His first connection with the theater was reputedly as holder of horses; that is, one of the stage crew, but a most inferior assignment. Thereafter he became an actor (perhaps at this time he met Ben Jonson), a writer, and a director. Such experience had its mark in the theatricality of his plays. We do know that he was established in London by 1592, when Robert Greene lamented in *A Groatsworth of Wit* (September, 1592) that professional actors had gained priority in the theater over university-trained writers like himself: "There is an upstart Crow, beautified with our feathers, that with his *Tygers hart wrapt in a Players hyde*, supposes he is as well able to bombast out a lanke verse as the best of you: and beeing an absolute *Iohannes fac totum* (Jack-of-all-trades), is in his owne conceit the onely Shake-scene in a countrey." An apology for Greene's ill-humored statement by Henry Chettle, the editor of the pamphlet, appeared around December 1592 in *Kind-Hart's Dream*.

Family Affairs

To return to the known details of family life, Shakespeare's son Hamnet was buried at Stratford on August 11, 1596; his father was given a coat of arms on October 20, 1596; and he purchased New Place (a refurbished tourist attraction today) on May 4, 1597. The London playwright obviously had not severed connections with his birthplace, and he was reflecting his new affluence by being known as William Shakespeare of Stratford-upon-Avon, in the County of Warwick, Gentleman. His father was buried in Stratford on September 8, 1601; his mother, on September 9, 1608. His daughter Susanna married Dr. John Hall on June 5, 1607, and they had a child named Elizabeth. His other daughter, Judith, married Thomas Quiney on February 10, 1616, without special licence, during Lent and was thus excommunicated. Shakespeare revised his will on March 25, 1616, and was buried on April 25, 1616 (according to the parish register). A monument by Gerard Janssen was erected in the Holy Trinity chancel in 1623 but many, like Milton several years later, protested:

> What needs my *Shakespeare* for his honour'd Bones,
> The labour of an age in piled Stone, . . .
> Thou in our wonder and astonishment
> Hast built thy self a live-long Monument.

Shakespeare's Writings

Order of Appearance

Dating of Shakespeare's early plays, while based on inconclusive evidence, has tended to hover around the early 1590's. Almost certainly it is his chronicles of Henry the Sixth that Philip Henslowe, an important theatrical manager of the day, referred to in his diary as being performed during March-May, 1592. An allusion to these plays also occurs in Thomas Nashe's *Piers Penniless His Supplication to the Devil* (August, 1592). Greene's quotation about a tiger is a paraphrase of "O tiger's heart wrapt in a woman's hide" from *Henry VI*, Part III.

The first published work to come from Shakespeare's hand was *Venus and Adonis* (1593), a long stanzaic poem, dedicated to Henry

Wriothesley, Earl of Southampton. A year later *The Rape of Lucrece* appeared, also dedicated to Southampton. Perhaps poetry was pursued during these years because the London theaters were closed as a result of a virulent siege of plague. The *Sonnets*, published in 1609, may owe something to Southampton, who had become Shakespeare's patron. Perhaps some were written as early as the first few years of the 1590's. They were mentioned (along with a number of plays) in 1598 by Francis Meres in his *Palladis Tamia*, and sonnets 138 and 144 were printed without authority by William Jaggard in *The Passionate Pilgrim* (1599).

There is a record of a performance of *A Comedy of Errors* at Gray's Inn (one of the law colleges) on December 28, 1594, and, during early 1595, Shakespeare was paid, along with the famous actors Richard Burbage and William Kempe, for performances before the Queen by the Lord Chamberlain's Men, a theatrical company formed the year before. The company founded the Globe Theatre on the south side of the Thames in 1599 and became the King's Men when James ascended the throne. Records show frequent payments to the company through its general manager John Heminge. From 1595 through 1614 there are numerous references to real estate transactions and other legal matters, to many performances, and to various publications connected with Shakespeare.

Order of Publication

The first plays to be printed were *Titus Andronicus* around February, 1594, and the garbled versions of *Henry VI*, Parts II and III in 1594. (Some scholars, however, question whether the last two are versions of *Henry VI*, Parts II and III, and some dispute Shakespeare's authorship.) Thereafter *Richard III* appeared in 1597 and 1598; *Richard II*, in 1597 and twice in 1598; *Romeo and Juliet*, in 1597 (a pirated edition) and 1599, and many others. Some of the plays appear in individual editions, with or without Shakespeare's name on the title page, but eighteen are known only from their appearance in the first collected volume (the so-called First Folio) of 1623. The editors were Heminge and Henry Condell, another member of Shakespeare's company. *Pericles* was omitted from the First Folio although it had appeared in 1609, 1611, and 1619; it was added to the Third Folio in 1664.

There was reluctance to publish plays at this time for various reasons; many plays were carelessly written for fast production; collaboration was frequent; plays were not really considered *reading* matter; they were sometimes circulated in manuscript; and the theatrical company, not the author, owned the rights. Those plays given individual publication appeared in a quarto, so named from the size of the page. A single sheet of paper was folded twice to make four leaves (thus *quarto*) or eight pages; these four leaves constitute one signature (one section of a bound book). A page measures about 6¾ in. x 8½ in. On the other hand, a folio sheet is folded once to make two leaves or four pages; three sheets, or twelve pages, constitute a signature. The page is approximately 8½ in. x 13⅜ in.

Authorized publication occurred when a company disbanded, when money was needed but rights were to be retained, when a play failed or ran into licensing difficulties (thus, hopefully, the printed work would justify the play against the criticism), or when a play had been pirated. Authorized editions are called good quartos. Piratical publication might occur when the manuscript of a play had circulated privately, when a member of a company desired money for himself, or when a stenographer or memorizer took the play down in the theater (such a version was recognizable by inclusion of stage directions derived from an eyewitness, by garbled sections, etc.). Pirated editions are called bad quartos; there are at least five bad quartos of Shakespeare's plays.

Authenticity of Works

Usually thirty-seven plays are printed in modern collections of Shakespeare's works but some recent scholars have urged the addition of two more: *Edward III* and *Two Noble Kinsmen*. A case has also been advanced, unconvincingly, for a fragment of the play on Sir Thomas More. At times, six of the generally-accepted plays have been questioned: *Henry VI*, Parts I, II and III, *Timon of Athens*, *Pericles* and *Henry VIII*. The first four are usually accepted today (one hopes all question concerning *Timon* has finally ended), but if Shakespeare did not write these plays in their entirety, he certainly wrote parts of them. Of course, collaboration in those days was commonplace. Aside from the two long narrative poems already mentioned and the sonnets (Nos. 1-152, but not Nos. 153-154), Shakespeare's poetic output is uncertain. *The Passionate Pilgrim* (1599) contains only five authenticated poems (two sonnets and three verses from *Love's Labour's Lost*); *The Phoenix and the Turtle* (1601) may be his, but the authenticity of *A Lover's Complaint* (appended to the sonnets) is highly questionable.

Who Was Shakespeare?

At this point we might mention a problem that has plagued Shakespeare study for over a century: who was Shakespeare? Those who would like to make the author of the plays someone else — Francis Bacon or the Earl of Oxford or even Christopher Marlowe (dead long before most of the plays were written) — have used the lack of information of Shakespeare's early years and the confusion in the evidence we have been examining to advance their candidate. But the major arguments against Shakespeare show the source of these speculators' disbelief to be in classconscious snobbery and perhaps in a perverse adherence to minority opinion. The most common argument is that no one of Shakespeare's background, lack of education, and lack of aristocratic experience could know all that the author knew. But study will reveal that such information was readily available in various popular sources, that some of it lies in the literary sources used for the play, and that Shakespeare was probably not totally lacking in education or in social decorum. The more significant question of style and tone is not dealt with — nor could it successfully be raised. Bacon, for example, no matter how much we admire his mind and his writings, exhibits a writing style diametrically opposite to Shakespeare's, a style most unpoetic and often flat. The student would be wise not to waste time rehashing these unfounded theories. No such question was raised in the seventeenth or eighteenth centuries, and no serious student of the plays today doubts that Shakespeare *was* Shakespeare.

Shakespeare's Plays

Exact dates for Shakespeare's plays remain a source of debate among scholars. The following serve only as a general frame of reference.

	COMEDIES	TRAGEDIES	HISTORIES
1591			Henry VI, Part I
1592	Comedy of Errors		Henry VI, Part II
1592	Two Gentlemen of Verona		Henry VI, Part III
1593	Love's Labour's Lost	Titus Andronicus	Richard III
1594			King John
1595	Midsummer Night's Dream	Romeo and Juliet	Richard II
1596	Merchant of Venice		
1596	Taming of the Shrew		
1597			Henry IV, Part I
1598	Much Ado About Nothing		Henry IV, Part II
1599	As You Like It	Julius Caesar	
1599	Merry Wives of Windsor		Henry V
1601	Twelfth Night	Hamlet	
1602	Troilus and Cressida		
1602	All's Well That Ends Well		
1604	Measure for Measure	Othello	
1605		King Lear	
1606		Macbeth	
1607		Timon of Athens	
1607		Antony and Cleopatra	
1608	Pericles		
1609		Coriolanus	
1610	Cymbeline		
1611	Winter's Tale		
1611	Tempest		
1613			Henry VIII

Shakespeare's England

The world of Elizabethan and Jacobean England was a world of growth and change. The great increase in the middle class, and in the population as a whole, demanded a new economy and means of liveli-

6

hood, a new instrument of government (one recognizing "rights" and changed class structure), a new social code and a broad base of entertainment. The invention of printing a century before had contributed to that broader base, but it was the theater that supplied the more immediate needs of the greatest numbers. The theater grew and along with it came less-educated, more money-conscious writers, who gave the people what they wanted: entertainment. But Shakespeare, having passed through a brief period of hack writing, proceeded to set down important ideas in memorable language throughout most of his career. His plays, particularly the later ones, have been analyzed by recent critics in terms of literary quality through their metaphor, verse-line, relationships with psychology and myth, and elaborate structure. Yet Shakespeare was a man of the stage, and the plays were written to be performed. Only this will fully account for the humor of a deadly serious play like *Hamlet* or the spectacle of a *Coriolanus*.

Life in London

During Shakespeare's early years there, London was a walled city of about 200,000, with seven gates providing access to the city from the east, north, and west. It was geographically small and crisscrossed by narrow little streets and lanes. The various wards each had a parish church that dominated the life of the close-knit community. To the south and outside were slums and the haunts of criminal types, and farther out were the agricultural lands and huge estates. As the population increased and the central area declined, the fashionable people of the city moved toward the west, where the palace of Westminster lay. Houses were generally rented out floor by floor and sometimes room by room. Slums were common within the city, too, though close to pleasant enough streets and squares. "Merrie Olde England" was not really clean, nor were its people, for in those days there were no sewers or drains except the gutter in the middle of the street, into which garbage would be emptied to be floated off by the rain to Fleet ditch or Moor ditch. Plague was particularly ravaging in 1592, 1593-94 (when the theaters were closed to avoid contamination) and 1603. Medical knowledge, of course, was slight; ills were "cured" by amputation, leeching, blood-letting and cathartics. The city was (and still is) dominated by St. Paul's Cathedral, around which booksellers clustered on Paternoster Row.

Religious Atmosphere

Of great significance for the times was religion. Under Elizabeth, a state church had developed; it was Protestant in nature and was called Anglican (or today, Episcopalian) but it had arisen from Henry VIII's break with the Pope and from a compromise with the Roman Catholics who had gained power under Mary Tudor.

The Church of England was headed by the Archbishop of Canterbury, who was to be an increasingly important figure in the early part of the seventeenth century. There were also many schismatic groups, which generally desired further departures from Roman Catholicism. Calvinists were perhaps the most numerous and important of the Protestant groups. The Puritans, who were Calvinist, desired to "purify" the church of ritual and certain dogmas, but during the 1590's they were lampooned as extremists in dress and conduct.

Political Milieu

During Shakespeare's lifetime there were two monarchs: Elizabeth, 1558-1603, and James I, 1603-1625. Elizabeth was the daughter of Henry VIII and Anne Boleyn, his second wife, who was executed in 1536. After Henry's death, his son by his third wife, Jane Seymore (died in 1537), reigned as Edward VI. He was followed by Mary Tudor, daughter of Henry's first wife, Catherine of Aragon. Mary was a Roman Catholic, who tried to put down religious dissension by persecution of both Protestants and Catholics. Nor did her marriage to Philip II of Spain endear her to the people.

Elizabeth's reign was troubled by many offers of marriage, particularly from Spanish and French nobles — all Roman Catholic — and by the people's concern for an heir to the throne. English suitors generally cancelled one another out by intrigue or aggressiveness. One of the most prominent was the Earl of Essex, Robert Devereux, who fell in and out of favor; he apparently attempted to take over the reins of control, only to be captured, imprisoned and executed in February, 1601. One claimant to the throne was Mary of Scotland, a Roman Catholic and widow of Francis II of France. She was the second cousin of Elizabeth, tracing her claim through her grandmother, who was Henry VIII's sister. Finally, settlement came with Elizabeth's acceptance of Mary's son as heir apparent, though Mary was to be captured, tried and executed for treason in 1587. Mary had abdicated the throne of Scotland in 1567 in favor of her son, James VI. His ascent to the throne of England in 1603 as James I joined the two kingdoms for the first time, although Scotland during the seventeenth century often acted independently of England.

Contemporary Events

Political and religious problems were intermingled in the celebrated Gunpowder Plot. Angry over fines that were levied upon those not attending Church of England services — primarily Roman Catholics — and offended by difficulties over papal envoys, a group of Catholics plotted to blow up Parliament, and James with it, at its first session on November 5, 1605. A cache of gunpowder was stored in the cellar, guarded by various conspirators, among them Guy Fawkes. The plot was discovered before it could be carried out and Fawkes, on duty at the time, was apprehended. The execution of the plotters and the triumph of the anti-Papists led in succeeding years to celebrations in the streets and the hanging of Fawkes in effigy.

Among the most noteworthy public events during these times were the wars with the Spanish, which included the defeat of the Spanish Armada in 1588, the battle in the Lowlands in 1590-1594, the expedition to Cadiz under Essex in 1596 and the expedition to the Azores (the Islands Expedition), also under Essex, in 1597. With trading companies especially set up for colonization and exploitation, travel excited the imagination of the people: here was a new way of life, here were new customs brought back by the sailors and merchants, here was a new dream world to explore.

In all, the years from around 1590 to 1601 were trying ones for English people, relieved only by the news from abroad, the new affluence and the hope for the future under James. Writers of the period frequently reflect, however, the disillusionment and sadness of those difficult times.

The Elizabethan Theater

Appearance

The Elizabethan playhouse developed from the medieval inn with its rooms grouped around a courtyard into which a stage was built. This pattern was used in The Theatre, built by James Burbage in 1576: a square frame building (later round or octagonal) with a square yard, three tiers of galleries, each jutting out over the one below, and a stage extending into the middle of the yard, where people stood or sat on improvised seats. There was no cover over the yard or stage and lighting was therefore natural. Thus performances were what we might consider late matinees or early evening performances; in summer, daylight continues in London until around ten o'clock.

Other theaters were constructed during the ensuing years: The Curtain in 1577, The Rose in 1587 (on Bankside), The Swan in 1595 (also Bankside) and Shakespeare's playhouse, The Globe, in 1599 (not far from The Rose). There is still some question about the exact dimensions of this house, but it seems to have been octagonal, each side measuring about 36 feet, with an over-all diameter of 84 feet. It was about 33 feet to the eaves, and the yard was 56 feet in diameter. Three sides were used for backstage and to serve the needs of the players. There was no curtain or proscenium, hence the spectators became part of the action. Obviously, the actors' asides and soliloquies were effective under these conditions.

There was no real scenery and there were only a few major props; thus the lines of the play had to reveal locations and movement, changes in time or place, etc. In this way, too, it was easier to establish a nonrealistic setting, for all settings were created in words. On either side of the stage were doors, within the flooring were trapdoors (for

9

entrances of ghosts, etc.), and behind the main stage was the inner stage or recess. Here, indoor scenes (such as a court or a bedchamber) were played, and some props could be used because the inner stage was usually concealed by a curtain when not in use. It might also have served to hide someone behind the ever-present arras, like Polonius in *Hamlet*. The "chamber" was on the second level, with windows and a balcony. On the third level was another chamber, primarily for musicians.

Actors

An acting company such as the Lord Chamberlain's Men was a fellowship of ten to fifteen sharers with some ten to twelve extras, three or four boys (often to play women's roles) who might become full sharers, and stagehands. There were rival companies, each with its leading dramatist and leading tragic actor and clown. The Lord Admiral's Men, organized in 1594, boasted Ben Jonson and the tragedian Edward Alleyn. Some of the rivalry of this War of the Theaters is reflected in the speeches of Hamlet, who also comments on the ascendancy and unwarranted popularity of the children's companies (like the Children of Blackfriars) in the late 1590's.

The company dramatist, of course, had to think in terms of the members of his company as he wrote his play. He had to make use of the physical features and peculiar talents of the actors, making sure, besides, that there was a role for each member. The fact that women's parts were taken by boys imposed obvious limitations on the range of action. Accordingly, we often find women characters impersonating men; for example, Robert Goffe played Portia in *The Merchant of Venice*, and Portia impersonates a male lawyer in the important trial scene. Goffe also played Juliet, and Anne in *Richard III*, and Oberon in *Midsummer Night's Dream*. The influence of an actor on the playwright can be seen, on the one hand, by noting the "humor" characters portrayed so competently by Thomas Pope, who was a choleric Mercutio in *Romeo*, a melancholic Jaques in *As You Like It*, and a sanguinary Falstaff in *Henry IV*, Part I; and by comparing, on the other hand, the clown Bottom in *Midsummer Night's Dream*, played in a frolicsome manner by William Kempe, with the clown Feste in *Twelfth Night*, sung and danced by Robert Armin. Obviously, too, if a certain kind of character was not available within the company, then that kind of character could not be written into the play. The approach was decidedly different from ours today, where the play almost always comes first and the casting of roles second. The plays were performed in a repertory system, with a different play each afternoon. The average life of a play was about ten performances.

History of the Drama

English drama goes back to native forms developed from playlets presented at Church holidays. Mystery plays dealt with biblical stories

10

such as the Nativity or the Passion, and miracle plays usually depicted the lives of saints. The merchant and craft guilds that came to own and produce the cycles of plays were the forerunners of the theatrical companies of Shakespeare's time. The kind of production these cycles received, either as moving pageants in the streets or as staged shows in a churchyard, influenced the late sixteenth-century production of a secular play: there was an intimacy with the audience and there was a great reliance on words rather than setting and props. Similar involvement with the stage action is experienced by audiences of the arena theater of today.

The morality play, the next form to develop, was an allegory of the spiritual conflict between good and evil in the soul of man. The *dramatis personae* were abstract virtues and vices, with at least one man representing Mankind (or Everyman, as the most popular of these plays was titled). Some modern critics see *Othello* as a kind of morality play in which the soul of Othello is vied for by the aggressively evil Iago (as a kind of Satanic figure) and passively good Desdemona (as a personification of Christian faith in all men). The Tudor interlude — a short, witty, visual play — may have influenced the subplot of the Elizabethan play with its low-life and jesting and visual tricks. In mid-sixteenth century appeared the earliest known English comedies, Nicholas Udall's *Ralph Roister Doister* and *Gammer Gurton's Needle* (of uncertain authorship). Both show the influence of the Roman comic playwright Plautus. Shakespeare's *Comedy of Errors*, performed in the 1590's, was an adaptation of Plautus' *Menaechmi*, both plays featuring twins and an involved story of confused identities. The influence of the Roman tragedian Seneca can be traced from Thomas Norton and Thomas Sackville in *Gorboduc* to *Hamlet*. Senecan tragedy is a tragedy of revenge, characterized by many deaths, much blood-letting, ghosts, feigned madness and the motif of a death for a death.

Shakespeare's Artistry

Plots

Generally, a Shakespearean play has two plots: a main plot and a subplot. The subplot reflects the main plot and is often concerned with inferior characters. Two contrasting examples will suffice: Lear and his daughters furnish the characters for the main plot of filial love and ingratitude, whereas Gloucester and his sons enact the same theme in the subplot; Lear and Gloucester both learn that outward signs of love may be false. In *Midsummer Night's Dream*, the town workmen (Quince, Bottom *et al.*) put on a tragic play in such a hilarious way that it turns the subject of the play — love so strong that the hero will kill himself if his loved one dies first — into farce, but this in the main plot is the "serious" plight of the four mixed-up lovers. In both examples Shakespeare has reinforced his points by subplots dealing with the same subject as the main plot.

11

Sources

The plots of the Elizabethan plays were usually adapted from other sources. "Originality" was not the sought quality; a kind of variation on a theme was. It was felt that one could better evaluate the playwright's worth by seeing what he did with a familiar tale. What he stressed, how he stressed it, how he restructured the familiar elements — these were the important matters. Shakespeare closely followed Sir Thomas North's very popular translation of Plutarch's *Life of Marcus Antonius*, for example, in writing *Antony and Cleopatra*; and he modified Robert Greene's *Pandosto* and combined it with the Pygmalion myth in *The Winter's Tale*, while drawing the character of Autolycus from certain pamphlets written by Greene. The only plays for which sources have not been clearly determined are *Love's Labour's Lost* (probably based on contemporary events) and *The Tempest* (possibly based on some shipwreck account from travellers to the New World).

Verse and Prose

There is a mixture of verse and prose in the plays, partially because plays fully in verse were out of fashion. Greater variety could thus be achieved and character or atmosphere could be more precisely delineated. Elevated passages, philosophically significant ideas, speeches by men of high rank are in verse, but comic and light parts, speeches including dialect or broken English, and scenes that move more rapidly or simply give mundane information are in prose. The poetry is almost always blank verse (iambic pentameter lines without rhyme). Rhyme is used, however (particularly the couplet), to mark the close of scenes or an important action. Rhyme also serves as a cue for the entrance of another actor or some off-stage business, to point to a change of mood or thought, as a forceful opening after a passage of prose, to convey excitement or passion or sentimentality and to distinguish characters.

Shakespeare's plays may be divided into three general categories, though some plays are not readily classified and further subdivisions may be suggested within a category.

The History Play

The history play, or chronicle, may tend to tragedy, like *Richard II*, or to comedy, like *Henry IV*, Part I. It is a chronicle of some royal personage, often altered for dramatic purposes, even to the point of falsification of the facts. Its popularity may have resulted from the rising of nationalism of the English, nurtured by their successes against the Spanish, their developing trade and colonization, and their rising prestige as a world power. The chronicle was considered a political guide, like the popular *Mirror for Magistrates*, a collection of writings showing what happens when an important leader falls through some error in his ways, his thinking or his personality. Thus the history play counseled the right path by negative, if not positive, means. Accordingly, it is difficult to call *Richard II* a tragedy, since Richard was wrong and his wrongness harmed his people. The political philosophy of Shakespeare's day seemed to favor the view that all usurpation was bad and should be corrected, but not by further usurpation. When that original usurpation had been established, through an heir's ascension to the throne, it was to be accepted. Then any rebellion against the "true" king would be a rebellion against God.

Tragedy

Tragedy in simple terms meant that the protagonist died. Certain concepts drawn from Aristotle's *Poetics* require a tragic hero of high standing, who must oppose some conflicting force, either external or internal. The tragic hero should be dominated by a *hamartia* (a so-called tragic flaw, but really an *excess* of some character trait, e.g., pride, or *hubris*), and it is this *hamartia* that leads to his downfall and, because of his status, to the downfall of others. The action presented in the tragedy must be recognizable to the audience as real and potential: through seeing it enacted, the audience has its passion (primarily suffering) raised, and the conclusion of the action thus brings release from that passion (*catharsis*). A more meaningful way of looking at tragedy in the Elizabethan theater, however, is to see it as that which occurs when essential good (like Hamlet) is wasted (through disaster or death) in the process of driving out evil (such as Claudius represents).

Comedy

Comedy in simple terms meant that the play ended happily for the protagonists. Sometimes the comedy depends on exaggerations of man's eccentricities — comedy of humors; sometimes the comedy is romantic and far-fetched. The romantic comedy was usually based on a mix-up in events or confused identity of characters, particularly by disguise. It moved toward tragedy in that an important person might die and the mix-up might never be unraveled; but in the nick of time something happens or someone appears (sometimes illogically or unexpectedly) and saves the day. It reflects the structure of myth by moving from happiness to despair to resurrection. *The Winter's Tale* is a perfect example of this, for the happiness of the first part is banished with Hermione's exile and Perdita's abandonment; tragedy is near when the lost baby, Perdita, cannot be found and Hermione is presumed dead, but Perdita re-appears, as does Hermione, a statue that suddenly comes to life. Lost identities are established and confusions disappear but the mythic-comic nature of the play is seen in the reuniting of the mother, Hermione, a kind of Ceres, with her daughter, Perdita, a kind of Proserpina. Spring returns, summer will bring the harvest, and the winter of the tale is left behind — for a little while.

What is it, then, that makes Shakespeare's art so great? Perhaps we see in it a whole spectrum of humanity, treated impersonally, but with kindness and understanding. We seldom meet in Shakespeare a weeping philosopher: he may criticize, but he criticizes both sides. After he has done so, he gives the impression of saying, Well, that's the way life is; people will always be like that — don't get upset about it. This is probably the key to the Duke's behavior in *Measure for Measure* — a most unbitter comedy despite former labels. Only in *Hamlet* does Shakespeare not seem to fit this statement; it is the one play that Shakespeare, the person, enters.

As we grow older and our range of experience widens, so, too, does Shakespeare's range seem to expand. Perhaps this lies in the ambiguities of his own materials, which allow for numerous individual readings. We meet our own experiences — and they are ours alone, we think — expressed in phrases that we thought our own or of our own discovery. What makes Shakespeare's art so great, then, is his ability to say so much to so many people in such memorable language: he is himself "the show and gaze o' the time."

TWELFTH NIGHT
Plot Summary

Viola and Sebastian, almost identical twins, were separated when their ship was wrecked during a great storm at sea. Each, thinking the other was dead, set out into the world alone, with no hope of being reunited.

The lovely and charming Viola was cast upon the shores of Illyria, where she was befriended by a kind sea captain. Together, they planned to dress Viola in men's clothing and have her take a job as a page in the household of young Duke Orsino. This course was decided upon because there was no chance of her entering the service of the Countess Olivia, a rich noblewoman of the duchy. Olivia, in deep mourning over the death of her young brother, would admit no one to her palace and would never think of interviewing a servant. So Viola, dressed in men's clothing, called herself Cesario and became the duke's personal attendant. Orsino, impressed by the youth's good looks and pert but courtly speech, sent him as his envoy of love to woo the Countess Olivia.

That wealthy noblewoman lived in a splendid palace with a servant, Maria, a drunken old uncle, Sir Toby Belch, and her steward, Malvolio.

Maria and Sir Toby were a happy-go-lucky pair who drank and caroused with Sir Andrew Aguecheek, an older nobleman who was in love with Olivia. In return for the grog supplied by Sir Andrew, Sir Toby was supposed to press Sir Andrew's suit of love with Olivia. Actually, however, Sir Toby never sobered up long enough to maintain his part of the bargain. All these affairs were observed with a great deal of disapproval by Malvolio, the ambitious, narrow-minded steward.

When Cesario arrived at the palace, Olivia finally decided to receive a messenger from Orsino. Olivia was instantly attracted to Cesario, and it was not love for Orsino that caused Olivia to listen so carefully. When Cesario left, the countess, feeling in a flirtatious mood, sent Malvolio after the page with a ring. With an abrupt shock, Viola, who enjoyed playing the part of Cesario, realized that Olivia had fallen in love with her in her disguise.

Meanwhile, Maria with Sir Toby and Sir Andrew decided to stop Malvolio's constant prying into their affairs. Maria devised a scheme whereby Malvolio would find a note, supposedly written by Olivia, in which she confessed her secret love for the steward and asked him to wear yellow stockings tied with cross garters and to smile continually in her presence. Malvolio, discovering the note, was overjoyed. Soon he appeared in his strange dress, smiling and bowing before the countess. Olivia, startled by the sight of her usually dignified steward behaving in such a peculiar fashion, decided he had lost his wits. Much to the amusement of the three conspirators, she had him confined to a dark room.

As the days went by in the duke's service, Viola fell deeply in love with the sentimental nobleman, but he had eyes only for Olivia and encouraged the page to renew his suit with the countess. When Cesario returned with another message from the duke, Olivia openly declared her love for the young page. Cesario insisted, however, that his was a heart that could never belong to any woman. So obvious were Olivia's feelings for Cesario that Sir Andrew became jealous. Sir Toby and Maria insisted that Sir Andrew's only course was to fight a duel with the page. Sir Toby delivered Sir Andrew's blustering challenge, which Cesario reluctantly accepted.

While these events were taking place, Sebastian, Viola's twin brother, had been rescued by Antonio, a sea captain, and the two had become close friends. When Sebastian decided to visit the court of Duke Orsino at Illyria, Antonio, although he feared that he might be arrested because he was the duke's enemy and had once fought a duel with Orsino, decided to accompany his young friend. Upon arrival in Illyria, Antonio gave Sebastian his purse for safekeeping, and the two men separated for several hours.

During his wanderings about the city Antonio happened upon the trumped-up duel between the unwilling Cesario and Sir Andrew. Mistaking the page for Sebastian, Antonio immediately went to the rescue of his supposed friend. When police officers arrived on the scene, one of them recognized Antonio and arrested him in the name of the duke.

Antonio, mistaking Viola in disguise for Sebastian, asked for the return of his purse, only to be surprised and hurt because the page denied all knowledge of the captain's money.

The real Sebastian, meanwhile, had been followed by Sir Andrew, who never dreamed that the young man was not the same Cesario with whom he had just been fighting. Egged on by Sir Toby and Maria, Sir Andrew engaged Sebastian in a duel and was wounded, along with Sir Toby. Olivia then interfered and had Sebastian taken to her home. There, having sent for a priest, she married the surprised but not unwilling Sebastian.

The officers were escorting Antonio past Olivia's house as Duke Orsino, accompanied by Cesario, appeared at the gates. Instantly, Orsino recognized Antonio and demanded to know why the sailor had returned to Illyria, a city filled with his enemies. Antonio explained that he had rescued and befriended the duke's present companion, Sebastian, and because of his deep friendship with the lad had accompanied him to Illyria despite the danger his visit involved. Then, pointing to Cesario, he sorrowfully accused the supposed Sebastian of violating their friendship by not returning his purse.

The duke was protesting against this accusation when Olivia appeared and greeted Cesario as her husband. The duke also began to think his page ungrateful, especially so since Cesario had been told to press Orsino's suit with Olivia. Just then, Sir Andrew and Sir Toby came running in looking for a doctor because Sebastian had wounded them. Seeing Cesario, Sir Andrew began to criticize him for his violence. Olivia dismissed the two older men quickly. As they left, the real Sebastian appeared and apologized for the wounds he had given them.

Spying Antonio, Sebastian joyfully greeted his friend. Antonio and the rest of the amazed group, unable to believe what they saw, stared from Cesario to Sebastian. Viola then revealed her true identity, explained her disguise, and told how she and her brother had been separated. The mystery cleared up, Sebastian and Viola affectionately greeted each other. The Duke, seeing that the page of whom he had grown so fond was in reality a woman, asked that Viola dress again in feminine attire. She was unable to do as he desired, she explained, because the kind sea captain to whom she had entrusted her own clothes was held in prison through the orders of Malvolio. This difficulty was cleared up quickly, for Olivia's clown, Feste, visited him in his confinement and returned with a long letter in which the steward explained the reasons for his actions. The plot against him revealed, Malvolio was released. Then followed the freeing of the sea captain, the marriage of Viola and Orsino, and also that of Sir Toby and Maria. Only Malvolio, unhappy in the happiness of others, remained upset.

Introduction

Date of Composition

The date of its composition, as of most of Shakespeare's plays, must be drawn from a mass of suppositions and indirect evidence. Since there is some likelihood that Francis Meres, in his *Palladis Tamia, Wit's Treasury* of 1598, listed all of Shakespeare's plays then written, we may assume that *Twelfth Night*, not mentioned there, had not yet been produced. An entry in the diary of John Manningham, under the date of February 2, 1601 (according to an old style, when the year ended on March 25; it was 1602 by our calendar), records that "At our feast we had a play called *Twelfth Night*, or *What You Will*, much like *The Comedy of Errors* or *Menaechmi* in Plautus, but most like and near to that in Italian called *Inganni*." As he goes on to recount the Malvolio story, there is no doubt that he is referring to Shakespeare's play, and thus he establishes the latest possible date for its composition.

Title

The title, *Twelfth Night*, which has no real bearing upon the story, may well have been given to the play because of a performance presented twelve days after Christmas, on January 6, the Feast of Epiphany, the culmination of the holiday festivities. Some scholars, indeed, think that the play was at first entitled *What You Will*, then given the other name after the January 6 performance.

Background of the Play

The most ingenious speculation along this line is that of Leslie Hotson. He points out that on Saint Stephen's Night (December 26) of the year 1600, Queen Elizabeth, then sixty-seven, learned that she was to be visited by the twenty-eight-year-old Don Virginio Orsino, Duke of Bracciano. He was an important figure, the son of Isabella de' Medici, and the nephew of Ferdinand I, Grand Duke of Tuscany, who had raised Don Virginio in his Pitti Palace in Florence. The Queen asked her Lord Chamberlain, Baron Hunsdon, "to make choyce of a play that shalbe best furnished with rich apparell, have great variety and change of musicke and daunces." From these words, Hotson resorts to "conjecture": that, instead of choosing a play, the Chamberlain commissioned Shakespeare to write one, and by the eleventh day thereafter he had ready, and presented for the enjoyment of Her Majesty and the distinguished Duke, the comedy *Twelfth Night*. And, "as a pretty compliment," the playwright named the Duke within the play Orsino. (Other scholars call the visiting Duke *Valentine* Orsino, and thus derive from him the names of the two characters in Shakespeare's play.) There is also a letter from the Duke to his Duchess, telling her he had been honored by the Queen with the spectacle of a "mixed comedy, with music and dances."

Enticing as this picture is, there is more than the difficulty of writing and rehearsing a play within eleven days that makes us hesitate to accept Hotson's conjecture. Although the Queen requested dances in the play in her command to Hunsdon, and dances were mentioned as part of the performance in the Duke's letter to his wife, Shakespeare's play has none. And what Hotson calls "a pretty compliment" was actually a considerable risk. How was the author to know that the young Duke would be pleased at finding his name applied to a mooning, melancholy, and somewhat spineless lord who makes a lightning switch of his professed devotion? Hotson also suggests that there are many similarities and suggestions that link the Queen with Olivia; but would the aging and sensitive Elizabeth be pleased to have herself shown in mistaken love of a woman, then patched up and passed off at the end on a johnny-come-lately second choice? The associations sound unlikely — and the punishment for an offending playwright was instant and severe. Jonson, Marston, and Chapman, for having collaborated on a play that rubbed a lord the wrong way, were imprisoned and sentenced to have their ears and noses cut off. Middleton, a little later, was put in jail because a Spaniard complained of his *A Game At Chess*. Shakespeare himself, by most accounts, had had to insert an apology in a play for having used the name Oldcastle; he changed it to Falstaff. He would be wary of a second intrusion.

The real Duke Orsino, we are told (like the real Shakespeare), had boy and girl twins, and it might be suggested that the twins in *Twelfth Night* were presented as an additional compliment to the Duke. Yet, valuable an ally as Tuscany might prove in the war with Spain, we still lack real proof that Shakespeare's play was part of the Duke's entertainment. We know so little of Shakespeare's life that it is tempting to magnify speculation into likelihood, then turn likelihood into fact.

First Folio, 1623

The first we actually see of *Twelfth Night* is in the First Folio collected edition of 1623. The manuscript seems to have been a good one, and in the play there are comparatively few obscure passages or disputed readings.

Sources

A number of earlier works have been mentioned as sources of the plot in *Twelfth Night*. Italian dramas present the confusion of twins, and the wooing by proxy wherein the lady falls in love with a disguised page. *Gl' Ingannati* ("*The Deceived*") was produced in Siena in 1531 and printed in 1538. Two similar plays, both called *Inganni*, appeared in 1562 and 1592. Cintio and Bandello wrote *novelles* with such plots; a loose adaptation of the latter's story of Apolonius and Silla is one of the eight tales in Barnaby Riche's *Farewell to the Military Profession*, 1581. This seems the closest direct source, except possibly for a Latin translation of *Gl' Ingannati*, called *Laelia* after the heroine, which was performed at Queen's College, Cambridge, in 1590 and 1598.

In none of these possible sources, however, do we find the persons of the subplot. Shakespeare may have drawn hints for the characters of Sir Andrew, the foolish gentleman; Maria, the witty servant; and Malvolio, the sanctimonious "Puritan," from the newly popular comedy of humors introduced by Jonson. But Shakespeare did not make them either extreme individuals or caricatures of types. Malvolio, for example, is a killjoy; but he has dignity and solidity, and, while he lacks humor, he also lacks the insincerity and the hypocrisy of the usual stage Puritan, such as Jonson's Rabbi Zeal-of-the-land Busy or Deacon Ananias. More, perhaps, than from outside sources, Shakespeare in this play drew upon and combined elements of his own earlier comedies. Thus, Feste fits into the development of the Shakespearean clown, between Touchstone of *As You Like It* and the Fool in *King Lear*. Sebastian's reception of Olivia's favor, "Or I am mad, or else this is a dream," is an echo of the words of Antipholus of Syracuse (Act II, Sc. 2, 214) in similar plight in *The Comedy of Errors*.

Suggestion of Melancholy

There is a suggestion of melancholy, or mournfulness, or the shadow of tragedy about many of Shakespeare's comedies. The first words of *The Comedy of Errors* are spoken by a man under sentence of death. The characters of *All's Well That Ends Well* all come upon us clothed in black. *The Merchant of Venice* begins with Antonio's saying,

"In sooth, I know not why I am so sad," and Portia's first words are a sigh, "By my troth, Nerissa, my little body is aweary of this great world." *Twelfth Night* opens with Orsino in love with melancholy; Olivia has lost a father and a brother, and Viola fears that her twin brother has been drowned. The mournful mood is dissipated by the sunshine of gaiety as the play moves on, but the "still, sad music of humanity" is a muted murmur, even to the final song.

Appearance and Reality

This dual awareness in the audience of the real world and the world of the play: the actual world of troubles and the dream world of joy is evoked by our noting how the characters are variously involved in self-deception. Orsino fashions a world of fancy out of being in love; Olivia seeks to shape a world of solitude by keeping alive mournful memories; Malvolio dreams of power and attractiveness, and creates a world that collapses about his shoulders. In another mood, this ironic discrepancy between appearance and actuality animates Shakespeare's tragedies. Hamlet declares, "I know not seems"; Troilus is taken in by the false glamor of Cressida; Macbeth confuses foul and fair; Othello deems "men honest that but seem to be so." What underlies their tragedies is brushed away in *Twelfth Night*, as by the magic of a song.

Popularity

Samuel Pepys, who visited a performance of *Twelfth Night* in 1663 because the King (Charles II) was there, wrote in his *Diary*: "A silly play, and not at all related to the name or day." A version by William Barnaby, called *Love Betrayed* or *The Agreeable Disappointment*, won no great success in 1703, and there were few performances of the original version during Samuel Johnson's time. Shakespeare's play grew in popularity with the nineteenth-century Romantics and a production at Daly's Theatre in London in 1894 saved the house after the disastrous failure of Tennyson's *The Foresters*. It has continued to be one of the most popular of Shakespeare's comedies, leading the critic W.A. Darlington to declare (in the New York *Times* of December 3, 1950) that, "to many people, myself most emphatically included, *Twelfth Night* is the nearest thing to a perfect comedy yet composed in English."

The Plots

1. The main plot, a love triangle between the Duke, Olivia and Viola, later involving Sebastian.

2. The three subplots which have no connection with the main plot, except that Viola is involved in both the main and one of the subplots. They add humor and contrast to the play, giving it a great variety of interests.

> a. The humiliation of Malvolio before Olivia, suggested by Maria and brought about by her forging a letter.

b. The imprisonment of Malvolio as a madman in a dark cell, suggested by Sir Toby and brought about by him, Maria and Fabian.

c. The duel between Sir Andrew and Viola, suggested by Sir Toby and Fabian to Sir Andrew to make him gain Olivia's favor. It is interrupted by Antonio and ends with the attack on Sebastian.

The Different Love Episodes

Different kinds of love are presented in *Twelfth Night*, as is common in all of Shakespeare's comedies.

ORSINO
He is a romantic and highly sentimental lover, more in love with love than a particular person. His love is like Romeo's passion for Rosaline before he meets Juliet, and it is meant to be satirized, although we are delighted by Orsino's eloquent poetry on love. He learns a truer, less sentimental love from Viola.

OLIVIA
She is passionate and falls in love at first sight. Her love is too strong to be curbed by her dignity, pride and modesty; she declares it openly — against the custom of the day; she rushes into marriage. Her marriage to Sebastian proves her blind haste, mistaking him for Viola.

VIOLA
She is truly in love with Orsino, not with love itself. She is selfless, serving Orsino's courtship to Olivia. She is loyal, steadfast, and less sentimental than Olivia.

SEBASTIAN
His love is natural, but not full-grown like that of Viola. He is passive in showing it and is willing to allow Olivia to take the initiative. His is also a love at first sight, and he does not stop to examine its depth.

SIR TOBY AND MARIA
The love between these two is not obvious, and it would appear that the attraction on Maria's side is Sir Toby's position and means, and on his side, Maria's wit and intelligence. They find in each other the grounds for good companionship and compatibility.

MALVOLIO
Malvolio's love is purely imaginary, the child of his vanity and conceit, and it ceases to exist as soon as he finds out how he has been duped. His mistress has what he secretly desires, wealth, position and

a good home, and because of these rather than anything else, he imagines that he is in love with her.

Critical Analysis of the Play

ACT I · SCENE 1

Summary

The play opens in the palace of the Duke of Illyria, an imaginary kingdom on the eastern shores of the Adriatic. A highly romantic comedy, *Twelfth Night* starts with a scene of sentimental romance. Duke Orsino enters with a group of courtiers bidding his musicians to play and soothe the exquisite love-melancholy in which he is steeped. He compares the music, rich, languorous and sweetly-sad, with the smell of violets in the wind. Quickly, the Duke grows tired of the music, and falls to philosophizing on the nature of love. Unlike the music, love does not sicken and bloat the appetite, but stays "quick and fresh." Its capacity is infinite, yet its desire for novelty is so great that no single object can satisfy it for long; it lives on variety. When Curio, one of his lords, suggests the idea of hunting for hart, the Duke reveals the reason of his love-melancholy, his consuming passion for Olivia. He compares himself to the hart, pursued by the hounds of his desire, tearing his heart, ever since his first view of the fair Countess. At this moment, Orsino's messenger, Valentine, returns from the latter's house. He reports that Olivia did not grant him a personal hearing of the Duke's suit, but notified him by her handmaid Maria of her decision to live in veiled seclusion for seven years. The reason for this strange vow is the death of her brother. The Duke's reaction is unexpectedly hopeful. Olivia's extravagant decision to "water once a day her chamber round with eye-offending brine" and keep her face veiled, paralleling his own luxuriant indulgence in love-sorrow, arouses his admiration. Such devotion to a dead kinsman gives him hope that her love will be far greater yet, once Cupid's arrow has struck her heart. The scene closes with the Duke expressing his desire to continue his thoughts of love amid the beds of flowers in his palace gardens.

Purposes

1. The main plot of the play, Orsino's courtship, is introduced.

2. The complications and the difficulties in store for the Duke are presented in Olivia's resolve to live secluded from the world for seven years.

3. The sentiment of love is introduced into the play from the start, in its most romantic form.

4. The reader is introduced into an atmosphere of high romance: the setting in Illyria, in the rich luxuriant south; the luxury and refine-

ment of the court; the music and flowers; the extravagant indulgence of Orsino and Olivia in exquisite love-thoughts and love-sorrow.

Notes

ORSINO

Nothing is said of the Duke's age, but he appears to be a young man, in love for the first time. He is looking for a wife, and has fastened on Olivia as most worthy of him. His tastes are refined and cultured; he whiles away his hours with the enjoyment of music and flowers. Though he has apparently seen little of Olivia, he considers himself desperately in love with her. His love is that of the first awakening; it is less fixed on one person but rather indulges in sentimental emotion. He is in love with love itself and tastes its joy and sadness as he tastes the refined pleasures of his court.

OLIVIA

We are prepared for a rather dazzling Olivia by the praise of Orsino. Her vow shows her to be a suitable heroine of a romantic, sentimental plot, and a female counterpart of Orsino.

LOVE AND MUSIC

Music and love go well together. The play begins with both, and continues the association until the final song. Since the love discussed in this scene is not mutual, the strains are mainly melancholy, with "a dying fall." The poetry is some of Shakespeare's loveliest. Donald Stauffer goes so far as to say that *"Twelfth Night* is the wedding of love and music."

SOUND AND FRAGRANCE

The association of sound and fragrance ("like the sweet sound That breathes upon a bank of violets") is not unique; indeed, Sir Toby, later (Act II, Sc. 3, 57-8), in discussing Feste's song, says, "To hear by the nose . . ." Some editors, nevertheless, quoting Sidney's *Arcadia* (1590): "Her breath is more sweet that a gentle south-west wind which comes creeping over flowrie fields," follow Alexander Pope in changing Shakespeare's *sound* to *south*: the sweet south wind.

LOVING AND BEING IN LOVE

Implied in this scene is a distinction between truly loving and being in love, a distinction which Shakespeare presses in other plays; plays as different in mood as *A Midsummer Night's Dream* and *Troilus and Cressida*. Being in love, or love-madness, was to the Elizabethans a kind of disease, a loss of self through sinking in a world of one's own creation. Loving was the ennobling of self through the recognition of and regard for the personality of the beloved.

INFLUENCE OF THE ORGANS

Picturing Olivia recovered from her mourning for her brother and wholly drawn to one lover, Orsino says, "when liver, brain, and heart, These sovereign thrones, are all supplied . . ." The Elizabethans believed that these organs, in the order given, were the seat of the passions, the intelligence, and the emotions.

HART IMAGERY

When Orsino states that, on seeing Olivia, "That instant was I turned into a hart," he is alluding to the classical Greek myth of the hunter Actacon who, coming upon the virgin goddess Artemis (Diana) as she bathed, was at once turned into a stag, and was pursued and torn to pieces by his own hounds. There is also, rather obviously, an implicit pun on *hart* and *heart*.

RHYMED COUPLETS

Lines 7 and 8, lines 11 and 12, and lines 40 and 41 at the end of the scene, form rhyming couplets. Indeed, the frequency of rhymed couplets in the play has led some critics to suggest an earlier date for its composition, before *Much Ado About Nothing* and *As You Like It*.

FOOD AND DRINK IMAGERY

Not only do food and drink play a large part in the comic scenes of the play, but they are frequently suggested in the imagery of the more romantic parts. Thus, here, we are told (line 29) of Olivia's tears that are intended to keep fresh the memory of her dead brother; we hear that she will use "brine . . . to season A brother's dead love." The image comes from the kitchen. Preserving by pickling is the image Shakespeare is using, and it may, by its deliberate incongruity, be intended to indicate the incongruity of seven years' retirement from life to mourn a brother.

ACT I · SCENE 2

Summary

This scene takes us to the coast of Illyria. There has been a shipwreck and Viola is on the shore with the captain of the ship and some sailors. Viola asks what country they are in and on being told it is Illyria, laments her separation from her brother, Sebastian, who must be in "Elysium." She fears that he is drowned but is reassured by the captain who maintains that he saw Sebastian strap himself to a mast. In gratitude for his comforting words she rewards him with gold.

The captain, who seems to know Illyria well, gives her information about the Duke Orsino who is "noble in nature and in name." Viola recalls that her father spoke of him but that he was then unwed. The captain tells her he is still not married but is seeking the hand of Olivia who has renounced the world for seven years to mourn the loss of her brother. Viola sees the similarity to her own situation, and would gladly go to live with her in service so that she too could renounce the world. However, the difficulty of speaking with her, presented by the captain, forces her to change her mind. Instead, she persuades the captain, after some flattering remarks, to present her to the Duke in the guise of a page, in order to become one of his servants. She assures the captain she could be useful, in that she could sing and talk to the Duke of "many sorts of music." The captain agrees, promising to keep the matter a secret.

Purposes

1. It introduces another of the main characters of the play, Viola, a second heroine.

2. It indicates the relationship between Viola and Sebastian and prepares for Sebastian's later introduction into the play.

3. It points out a certain similarity between Viola and Olivia, which Viola perceives and which draws her to Olivia.

4. It discloses Viola's plot to enter (disguised) into the Duke's service, and forecasts the complications that will arise from it.

Notes

VIOLA

She appears to be a wealthy gentlewoman whose father was acquainted with Orsino the Duke. She is concerned over the loss of her brother and sees in her state a similarity with that of Olivia's. The swift way in which she puts from her mind (for the time) her brother's fate, and sets about arranging for her future, and the ingenious devices to get herself into the Duke's service show her to be a person of strong character, intelligent and quick-witted. She feels that with her knowledge of music she could help the love-lorn ruler and become valuable in his service.

THE CAPTAIN

He serves here as a means of relating Sebastian's fate and the conditions in Illyria, as well as being the instrument by which Viola is introduced to the Duke's household. He is a rather garrulous man and eagerly helps Viola, whose charm wins her his sympathy.

EUNUCHS

In order to preserve the pure soprano of a singing boy, it was the practice in late Renaissance Europe, especially in Italy, to castrate such a lad before his voice had changed. (In the Near East, the male guards and attendants of the harem were also eunuchs.) The practice in Italy seems to have begun at about Shakespeare's time; the first eunuch to sing in the Pope's chapel performed in the year 1600. The practice lasted well into the nineteenth century, being finally forbidden by Pope Leo XIII, who died in 1903.

REFERENCE TO ARION
The First Folio reference to *Orion* (line 15) is unanimously changed to *Arion*, a semi-mythical poet who was thrown overboard by sailors that sought his wealth. Charmed by the song they allowed him to sing before heaving him over (one version says he leapt overboard to escape their knives), a dolphin bore him to safety on its back. (The story is mentioned in Virgil's *Eclogues* [8, 56].) In the play, the captain is describing Sebastian, tied to a mast in the sea:

> Where, like Arion on the dolphin's back,
> I saw him hold acquaintance with the waves
> So long as I could see.

VIOLA'S MOTIVES
Some critics have suggested that Viola, remembering that her father had spoken well of Duke Orsino, and hearing that he is still a bachelor, decides at once to win his heart. Others deny this vehemently. A beautiful, high-bred girl, alone in a strange country, she is seeking a proper course of action. At the Duke's bachelor court there can be no place for her; she therefore will go to the court of the Duke's beloved, also an orphan maiden mourning a brother. It is only after she is told that there is no way of access to Olivia that she determines to dress as a boy and seek service with the Duke.

DROWNING THEME
Viola is rescued from drowning in the sea. There are more references to drowning in this play than in any other of Shakespeare's except *The Tempest*. In a sense, we may say that one of its major themes is rescue from drowning. Sir Toby and Sir Andrew are drowning in the sea of drunken self-gratification; Malvolio in the sea of self-love; and Olivia and Orsino in the sea of sentimentalism.

ACT I · SCENE 3

Summary
Both the setting and tone of Scene 3 present a strong contrast to the romance of the preceding scenes. From the world of the love-sick Duke and from the wild sea coast, from romantic vows and disguises, we are brought into Olivia's house by the back door, so to speak. To heighten the suspense, Olivia does not appear as yet; instead, a scene of broad comedy takes place in her house. Sir Toby Belch, Olivia's uncle, enters followed by Maria, Olivia's attendant or "Handmaid." Sir Toby

complains of Olivia's undue grief over her brother's death and is in turn criticized by Maria. We hear from Maria that Olivia is distressed at Sir Toby's vulgar drinking and noise-making till late into the night. Sir Toby boastingly refuses to mend his ways. Maria complains about a new companion of his, Sir Andrew Aguecheek, a "foolish knight." Sir Toby defends his friend whom he wishes to court Olivia: he speaks of his height, wealth, skill with the viola-de-gamba, and knowledge of languages. Maria, unimpressed, calls the knight a wastrel, fool, a quarreler and coward. Sir Toby, with deliberate perverseness persists in his good opinion of Sir Andrew, and swears that he will drink to his niece as long as any drink is left.

At this moment, Sir Andrew Aguecheek comes into the house. He foolishly addresses Maria, as "Good Mistress Accost" mistaking Sir Toby's introduction of "accost Sir Andrew accost." When Maria turns to leave, Sir Andrew is further put out by her keen verbal wit in playing on his words, "fools in hand." Sir Toby cheers up the shamefaced knight by proposing some wine, though both appear half-drunk already. After a sad admission of his foolishness, blaming his beef-eating for it, and his ignorance of the arts, Sir Andrew states that he wishes to go home, as his suit to Olivia is not prospering. Sir Toby Belch persuades him that there is hope for him yet, since Olivia will not marry the Duke or anyone above her in age, station or wit, and so Sir Andrew agrees to stay a month longer enjoying drinking, masques, revels and other pleasures of a wealthy gentleman. He boasts of his proficiency in dancing. Sir Toby feeds his vanity by praising his skill and the shape of his leg "formed under the star of a galliard," or dance. The scene ends with Sir Andrew dancing, noisily applauded by Sir Toby.

Purposes

1. It introduces some of the chief characters of the subplot, Sir Toby Belch, Sir Andrew Aguecheek and Maria.

2. It displays a broad, farcical humor in the ranting of Sir Toby, the folly of Sir Andrew and the sharp tongue of Maria, the "fair shrew."

3. Contrasting with the sentiment and romance of the first scenes, it adds to the variety of the play by the use of buffoonery and occasional vulgarity.

4. The reference to Olivia's refusal to marry above her rank prepares the reader for coming difficulties in the Duke's suit.

5. Permits a time lapse for dramatic credibility between Scene 2 and Scene 4.

Notes

SIR TOBY BELCH

As his last name indicates, he is an outstanding drinker. He is, despite his common-sounding name and his ways, Olivia's uncle and guardian, the relation of the high-minded, refined Countess; and Sir Toby is characteristic of the mixture of romance and earthy comedy in the play. Sir Toby appears to be in early middle-age, probably in his late thirties. He is loud, boisterous and common, fondest of drinking and amusement. He is intelligent even in his spells of intoxication, and has a keen sense of humor: as seen in his rather clumsy use of puns; his humorous use of foreign words ("castiliano vulgo" and "pourquoi"); his bantering with Sir Andrew after Maria's departure; and his enjoyment of Sir Andrew's capers. He loves quarreling with Maria, in good humored fashion. As his part in the scene anticipates, he is to play a leading role in the subplot with Maria. He is duping Sir Andrew out of as much money as he can — his real purpose in inviting Sir Andrew to the house.

THE GULL

Sir Andrew is the complete simpleton, the butt or *gull* of every joke, too innocent even to know he's being laughed at. He is such a person as is held up to laughter in Dekker's *The Gull's Hornbook* (1609), a satirical picture of the fops of the day, which was printed in the guise of an instruction book on how to behave like a gallant. Notice that Shakespeare has us first meet the two knights under circumstances that will hardly admit our approval of them. Later, we may sympathize with Sir Toby's joy in life as opposed to the joylessness of Malvolio, but we are here forewarned against too hearty approval of the revelling knight.

MARIA'S RANK

Maria must not be mistaken for a mere servant. She speaks here with authority. Olivia later (Act I, Sc. 5, 162) refers to her as "my gentlewoman." Just as a young noble might be sent to a grander house to serve as page and to learn courtly behavior, so a young woman might be sent as lady-in-waiting, to learn courtly etiquette. The especially favored one became maid of honor to the Queen. Thus, when Sir Toby, at the play's end, marries Maria, there is no sense of a difference in their station.

USE OF VERSE AND PROSE

This scene is in prose, as indeed is about two-thirds of the play. The scenes that are all in prose present some combination of the characters Malvolio, Sir Toby, Sir Andrew, Maria, and Feste. Other scenes, in verse, may turn to prose for special effects, as Act I, Scene 5, when Viola-Cesario asks which is Olivia, so as not to waste the studied speech. (In Act III, Scene 1, Viola and Feste talk in prose; then she muses alone in verse. When Sir Toby and Sir Andrew enter, all three speak in prose again until the men go; then Viola and Olivia speak verse until the end of the scene.) The main movement of the play, more sentimental than comic, is in verse.

The use of prose makes the numbering of lines somewhat arbitrary,

In checking a reference in an edition of the play, one must be prepared for some discrepancies.

"CASTILIANO VULGO!"

Scholars have wondered what Sir Toby means by the exclamation *Castiliano vulgo!* (line 46). Some suggest that the allusion is to Spanish ducats: Toby is after Sir Andrew's money. Others, e.g., J. Dover Wilson, read it as *Castiliano voglio* ("I want some Castilian"); they interpret *Castilian* as a fine wine. Still others think the phrase is a command to Maria to put on a Castilian countenance, a grave face, at the approach of Sir Andrew Aguecheek. This, they declare, is borne out by Sir Toby's announcement, for he says, "Here comes Sir Andrew Auge-*face*." But some scholars believe that the expression, like others of Sir Toby's, defies definition; it is merely a bacchanalian cry, a ringing sound for a drinking bout — a call, not to arms, but to cups, at the approach of his drinking companion.

PUNS

There is much punning and double meaning in this scene. When Maria bids Sir Andrew bring his hand to the buttery bar — literally, the ledge on the half-door of a pantry, on which a tankard might be placed — she is giving him a flirtatious invitation. When Sir Andrew states, "I would I had bestowed that time in the tongues that I have in fencing, dancing, and bearbaiting," Sir Toby deliberately confuses *tongues* (languages) and *tongs* (for curling the hair). Then, he plays on *distaff*; he says he hopes that a woman will give Sir Andrew a venereal disease and make his hair fall off. When Sir Andrew, speaking of a dance step, says, "I can cut a caper," Sir Toby transfers the reference to a caper sauce, and says, "I can cut the mutton to it."

MISTRESS MALL

Paintings, until recent times, often had a curtain before them instead of a glass; we see one drawn aside in Browning's poem, *My Last Duchess*. But who is Mistress Mall, whose picture, Sir Toby says, was "like to take dust?" Several women have been suggested. Among them, the notorious Mary Frith, known as Mall Cutpurse; Middleton and Dekker wrote a comedy, *The Roaring Girl*, or *Moll Cut-Purse*, produced in 1611. But ten years earlier, the probable date of the composition of *Twelfth Night*, she was not so well known. Some critics, with less likelihood, suggest that she is the Maria of the play, but there is no reason to think Olivia would have her maid's portrait hanging. Others mention the disreputable Mall Fowler, who plotted with her lover to get rid of her husband, and in a crowded courtroom was found guilty, just before the play was written. Leslie Hotson, who believes that Malvolio is a travesty of Sir William Knollys, Comptroller of the Queen's Household, declares therefore, that Mall is the Queen's Maid of Honor Mary Fitton. The elderly Sir William was married, but in love with the vixen Mary; he asked her to promise to marry him when his wife died. At the time, Mary was dallying with the Earl of Pembroke, Lord Chamberlain (to whom, with his brother, the First Folio was dedicated). In December, 1600, Mary was six months' pregnant by the Earl; the next month she was dismissed from court. According to Hotson, *Mal volio* meant both "evil desire" and "I want Mall." In opposition to this notion, it may be pointed out that Malvolio is seeking the hand, not of Maria, but of his mistress, Olivia (who Hotson suggests represents Elizabeth, as "Olive," Princess of Peace). Still other critics sensibly shrug off the question of Mall's identity. Mary, of which Mall is a diminutive, is the most frequent of all women's names; and Mistress Mall may well be mentioned, like Master Tom, or Jack Robinson, without any particular person in mind.

SIGNS OF THE ZODIAC
At the close of the scene is a jest the Elizabethan audience would at once have grasped. The signs of the zodiac were often named around a representation of the human body, with lines from the names to the parts of the body astrologically under their influence. This figure may still be seen in *The Farmer's Almanac*.

> *Sir Toby.* Were we not born under Taurus?
> *Sir Andrew.* Taurus! That's sides and heart.
> *Sir Toby.* No, sir, it is legs and thighs.

Andrew's ignorance Shakespeare no doubt intended as ignorance. Sir Toby's misplacement is perhaps a satirical allusion to Andrew's vaunted talents as a dancer, and also bears a sexual implication. Taurus, in astrology, governs the neck and throat, and that sign is certainly appropriate to the boozy Sir Toby Belch.

ACT I · SCENE 4

Summary
We are returned to the Duke's palace. In the lapse of time since the Duke's first appearance, Viola has entered his service under the name of Cesario. Valentine is talking to the new page; he congratulates him on his quick rise in the Duke's favor and the preferences he is given by Orsino, though he has been with him only three days. Taking up Valentine's phrase "if the Duke continue these favors toward you," Viola slyly asks if the Duke is inconstant in his affections and is told that he is not. The Duke enters, drawing Viola aside to send to Olivia. He tells the new page to wait at her door, until she is admitted. Viola objects that her errand will be useless, if Olivia is as abandoned in her grief as rumor has it. Orsino tells her to persist and do whatever has to be done to get in to see Olivia. He further instructs Viola to plead his love suit

with feeling, adding that Viola's youth makes her a better love messenger than would be an older or graver man. Viola's objection to this is overruled by the Duke who comments on the girlish charms of the page, her red lips and sweet womanly voice. He sends Viola off with several attendants promising to reward her if she is successful, and withdrawing to solitude, "since he is best when least in company." Viola promises to do her best, but in an aside she reveals that she has already fallen in love with the Duke.

Purposes

1. It shows Viola successful in her plan announced in Scene 2; she has won the Duke's full confidence and favor.

2. The main plot with the Duke, Olivia and Viola is complicated by Viola's love for the Duke. The triangle is beginning to form.

3. The meeting between Olivia and Viola is anticipated.

4. An element of dramatic irony is created by Viola's situation when forced to further the suit of Orsino to her rival and keep up her disguise, while the Duke is already unconsciously falling in love with her.

Notes

VIOLA

Her quick success with the Duke is proof of her resourcefulness, intelligence and charm. Her quick love for the Duke shows her deep, affectionate nature. She attempts, with slight persistence, to convince the Duke that her errand to Olivia will be in vain, since she will not be admitted and if she is admitted will not know what to say to the Countess. She shows her loyalty in going to Olivia and suffering in silence through her love for the Duke. Of her appearance, we are told that she is soft, gentle and lovely even in male disguise.

ORSINO

He is still bent on his pursuit of Olivia though already moved to praise the charm of Viola to whom he has opened "the book even of my secret soul." He is generous and noble, promising Viola to reward her richly. Strangely enough, he, like his courtiers, has not penetrated Viola's superficial disguise, yet his affection and confidence in her prepare for his later sudden change of heart.

UNAWARENESS AND UNREALITY

Here is the first sharp conflict between appearance and reality. After the first two scenes of the play, there is not one scene without a character in some way unaware of what we or other characters know. In Scene 3, Sir Andrew does not recognize that he is the butt of the others' wit and that he is being swindled by Sir Toby. But here the dramatic irony is more striking, as the Duke unwittingly sends, to woo for him, a woman who loves him.

The lack of contact with reality and the false sentimentalism of both Orsino and Olivia is implied in the lady's attempt to shelter herself; it is here paralleled by the Duke's remark, "I myself am best When least in company."

Unlike the dominating Rosalind of *As You Like It*, who has a high time in her male attire, Viola — as the Duke's words imply — cannot disguise her essential femininity, and her masquerade is increasingly a source of embarrassment and a burden.

VALENTINE
The Duke's attendant, Valentine, is appropriately named for the mood of love. It was a valentine that (in Scene 1) the Duke first sent to Olivia, and it was Valentine that delivered it.

ACT I · SCENE 5

Summary
After the first four scenes which serve to introduce the main characters separately, we are plunged in this scene into the increasing complications of the main plot. Several members of the Countess' household, the fool Feste, the steward Malvolio, and Olivia herself are introduced.

At the start of the scene, Maria is seen talking to the Clown. He has just returned to the house after an apparently lengthy absence, and will not tell Maria where he has been. Maria threatens him with Olivia's displeasure, but Feste replies that he is not afraid to be hanged by Olivia, for he need fear no "colours," playing on the meaning of military "colours" and the hangman's "collar" or noose. When Maria points out to him that her mistress may fire him, he answers that summer will bear it out. He slyly remarks that "many a good hanging prevents a bad marriage," and teases Maria for her efforts to make Sir Toby stop drinking. Maria is embarrassed and uses the approach of Olivia to leave.

Olivia enters with her steward Malvolio. She asks to have the fool removed; when Feste asks to have the lady removed she calls him boring and dishonest. The Clown sets about to prove to her that, if he is either, he can improve, and then proceeds to prove Olivia a fool. He does it by showing to her the folly of mourning a brother in heaven, and Olivia, impressed by his verbal skill, turns to Malvolio to question him about the fool. The steward savagely retorts that "infirmity that decays the wise, doth ever make the better fool." The Clown wishes him speedy weakness to increase his folly and cites Sir Toby Belch as taking not him but Malvolio for a fool. Malvolio continues in a bitter denunciation of clowns and of those that enjoy their clowning as mere "fools' zanies."

Olivia accuses Malvolio of self-love and surliness; to her the Clown's joking is harmless and delightful. The Clown wishes her blessings from the god of lies for speaking well of fools.

At this point Maria returns and announces a young gentleman. She does not know him but says that Sir Toby is holding him back at the gate. Olivia sends her to remove Sir Toby, asks Malvolio to find out if it is a messenger from the Duke, and tells the Clown that he is no longer amusing, but rather boring. Sir Toby enters in his usual half-drunken condition, blaming his hiccups on the pickled herring he has eaten. Olivia sends the fool after him to get him out of his condition. Malvolio returns to report failure. The stranger at the gate refuses to move; he has an answer ready for anything that Malvolio may say. Growing curious, Olivia asks what he is like. Malvolio describes him as halfway between boy and man like a half-ripe apple or pea pod, good looking and sharp in speech. Olivia calls for Maria and veils herself; she wishes to listen to one more suit from Orsino.

Viola enters and asks for the lady of the house. She starts on an elaborate speech learned by heart, stopping again to inquire which is Olivia, since she does not wish to waste her speech on the wrong person. Asked where she comes from, she refuses to tell, as her part does not provide for such a question. To Olivia's question as to whether she is an actor, she states "I'm not that I play," implying for the audience her female identity unknown to Olivia. Olivia admits at last that she is the Countess. Viola returns to her speech but is asked by Olivia to drop the feigned praise and come to the point of her mission, or else to leave after her insolent waiting at the gate. She says that she brings peace not war, and desires to speak to the Countess privately. Viola's attendants and Maria are dismissed. Olivia asks for the "text" of Viola's "divinity," or solemn message. To Viola's reply, "most sweet lady," she counters that it is a comforting doctrine. Viola says that her text lies in Orsino's bosom, and Olivia, continuing the extended play of words on "divinity" asks in which chapter of his bosom. To Viola's, "in the first of his heart," she replies that it is heresy to her and asks if Viola has anything further to say. Viola wishes to see her rival's face and though Olivia knows that she has no authority from the Duke for her request she unveils her face. Viola praises her beauty, if it be real. She calls Olivia cruel for choosing to remain unmarried and possibly die without leaving the copy or heir of her beauty. Olivia replies that she will not be so cruel as to have her beauty recorded for posterity in "diverse schedules," or inventories, and asks if Viola's errand consists of praising her. Viola calls her proud, hard-hearted, but very beautiful; she speaks of the Duke's love, stating that even Olivia's beauty is not too great an object for it. Olivia asks about the nature of his love and Viola gives a brief account of highly charged passion, "adorations, fertile tears, with groans that thunder love, with sighs of fire." Olivia insists that Orsino knows her answer. She cannot love the Duke but she calls him virtuous, noble, youthful, blameless, wealthy, cultured and handsome. Viola, amazed at Olivia's coldness towards Orsino says that were she Orsino she would never understand such cruelty. She would build a willow hut at Olivia's gate and sigh for her, write songs and sing them "in the dead of night," call out Olivia's name and do everything to move Olivia's heart to pity. Olivia replies, "you might do much," impressed by Viola's fervor. She asks her origin; Viola will not disclose it, except to say that she is of noble birth though fallen in fortunes. Olivia sends her off to tell Orsino not to call again, unless Viola should return to tell how the Duke takes her answer. She offers Viola money. The page refuses it saying the compensation is due to Orsino not to her. She leaves, wishing Olivia may love a man as hard-hearted as herself who will spurn her love as she spurns Orsino's.

Olivia stays after Viola's departure, repeating her words about her gentle origin. She admits to herself that the page is truly noble in speech, looks, figure, deeds and soul. She has fallen in love with Viola whose charm subtly overcomes her decision to remain in solitude for seven years. She decides to let events take their course and calls for Malvolio. She sends him after the messenger to return a ring which he supposedly left behind. She tells Malvolio to force the ring on the page and to ask him to let the Duke know that Olivia cannot be won with rings. She also orders Malvolio to tell the messenger (Cesario) that he could return the next day to know her reasons for refusing the Duke. At the close of the scene, Olivia confesses to herself that she does not know what to do and decides to let fate show its force, being unable to follow a set course of her own.

Purposes

1. It introduces Olivia (in person) in several situations after the preparation of the previous scenes.

2. It brings Viola face to face with her rival, making her a central figure in the play.

3. It complicates the main plot by Olivia's falling in love with Viola. The triangle is complete.

4. It prepares for a further meeting of the two, by Malvolio's errand.

5. It introduces two important characters in the subplot, Feste and Malvolio.

6. It brings the two plots together in a mixed scene of comedy and romance.

Notes

THE CLOWN AND THE FOOL
Although the list of characters and the line-indications refer to Feste as a clown, he is really something quite different, the court fool.

The clown is a rustic, usually a simpleton; his humor comes, as it were, in spite of himself; he is as often butt as buffoon. The fool is a wit, a professional jester, whose liberties with his master are privileged, and who dares prick the follies of his superiors. As Feste puts it, "I wear not motley in my brain." It may be that Shakespeare changed the quality of his comic figures because a new player had come into his acting company; it is likely that his artistic growth accounts for the change. First Touchstone in *As You Like It*, then Feste, here, move with a different spirit from the rustics, a spirit most fully developed in the Fool of *King Lear*. The Fool sees through the excesses that surround him; in this scene he tries to make Olivia put her mourning into proper perspective.

MARIA
Feste's sly remark, "If Sir Toby would leave drinking, thou wert as witty a piece of Eve's flesh as any in Illyria," is our first hint that Maria may have a special interest in Sir Toby.

OLIVIA
Olivia is effectively drawn. She recognizes the excesses of Sir Toby and of Malvolio, pinpointing the latter's affectation in one word, "self-love." She observes Malvolio's faults objectively. Maria sees them also, but with intense dislike, partly, perhaps, because of her designs upon Sir Toby. Olivia's innate gentleness is shown in her response to, and defense of, Feste's jesting; and the stages of her feeling for Cesario, as it develops from a casual interest to a hopeless love, are a superb capsule of unknowing courtship. The break from her decision to maintain seven years of mourning thus becomes, not merely creditable, but credible.

VIOLA
The courtesy, innate gentleness, and decency of Viola peep through her disguise as, despite her love for Orsino, she faithfully presses his suit upon Olivia. Thus, she refuses the proffered purse with the reminder, "My master, not myself, lacks recompense." On the other hand, it must be observed that Olivia, though sweet and sentimental, is also a practical woman (does she not run a large household?). As soon as she takes an interest in Cesario, she inquires about his family. Alone, she reassuringly repeats the page's words, "I am a gentleman," before she allows herself the utterance of her love.

USE OF PROSE AND POETRY
This scene begins with prose, which continues until a few lines after Cesario and Olivia are alone. Then "Nature's sweet and cunning hand" is revealed not only in Olivia's countenance but in Shakespeare's versification, which spontaneously employs subtleties of style to add beauty to meaning. In the very first verses, alliteration appears: "'Tis *b*eauty truly *b*lent," then draws the counterpoint of inner rhyme:

35

> If you will *lead* these *graces* to the *grave*
> And *leave* the world no copy.

(This argument for having children also appears in Shakespeare's poem *Venus and Adonis*, and in the first group of his *Sonnets*.) The last four lines of the scene make two rhymed couplets, which tie together Olivia's thought that Fate has tied her to Cesario.

MALVOLIO

Olivia's steward is to play a very important part in the subplot. He is grave and surly in behavior, with an exaggerated sense of his own importance in the household. He detests gaiety and wit; his solemn behavior masks a heavy mind and spirit, though he does not lack intelligence. He hates the Clown for his obvious intelligence and cleverness under the guise of folly. His reply to Olivia's question as to what he thinks of Feste is savage and rude; he scores a temporary victory over Feste. Nobody likes him; the servants resent his overbearing manner. Olivia respects him as a steward, but she criticizes his self-love, "distempered appetite," or poisoned bitter temper, and his lack of humor. He rather grudgingly concedes Viola's good looks, but compares her to a green apple or unripe pea pod and stresses her ill-manner at the gate. Malvolio is shown to be sufficiently unpleasant in this scene to prepare for his later role as the butt of ridicule of Maria, Sir Toby and Feste.

ACT II · SCENE 1

Summary

Sebastian, Viola's brother, saved by Antonio, weeps that his twin sister, who greatly resembled him, is drowned. He thanks Antonio for his help, but bids him farewell, so that his own bad luck won't spread to the friendly captain. Sebastian heads for Duke Orsino's court. Although Antonio has many enemies there, he has been so drawn to the young Sebastian that he decides to follow him and see if he can be of service.

Purposes

1. It introduces Viola's twin brother, Sebastian, into Illyria.

2. It prepares for the confusion of their identities by stating their similarity of looks.

Notes

TWINS' RESEMBLANCE
Shakespeare accepts the notion that a male and female twin can be so like one another as to cause confusion. In life, identical twins are

36

always of the same sex. In the play, Shakespeare stresses their resemblance by having Viola come in immediately after Sebastian, dressed just like her brother.

This scene creates a break in the order of events. In the preceding scene, Olivia has sent Malvolio after Viola; in the scene that follows this one he overtakes her. But here, in between, we are taken to the coast. Shakespeare thus informs us that Viola's twin is alive, right after we learn that Olivia has fallen in love with the disguised Viola. Hence, when Viola, in the next scene, comes to the conclusion that Olivia has fallen in love with her, we already — if we know how to shuffle the cards — can tell how the game will end. And we are the charmed holders of the top secret. For while only Viola-Cesario shares with the audience the knowledge that she is a woman and is in love with Orsino, not even Viola knows that her twin brother is alive and on his way to Orsino's court. Thus, we have the pleasure of watching the characters in the play and enjoying our awareness of their ignorance. The end of such a play, as of most comedies, is easy to guess; it has been succinctly described: Boy Gets Girl. Perhaps — and not merely because the play may have been written in leap year — it would be more accurate to say Girl Gets Boy. We know the end; the playwright's problem is to keep us interested until that happy culmination comes; and one of his chief devices, one which Shakespeare exploits in rich variety, is to have us watch the things that occur because of the different levels of awareness among the characters. *Twelfth Night* abounds in such differences.

ACT II · SCENE 2

Summary

Malvolio, overtaking Cesario, bids the page to take back Orsino's ring, tell his master his cause is hopeless, and never come again — except to report how Orsino takes the news. Viola replies: "She took the ring of me. I'll none of it." Whereupon Malvolio retorts, "Come, sir, you peevishly threw it to her, and her will is it should be so returned." He tosses it to the ground, and goes.

Viola recognizes that the ring is a love-token intended for Cesario. She reflects:

> Poor lady, she were better love a dream.
> Disguise, I see thou art a wickedness . . .

She pictures the circle of intertangled lovers she, Olivia, and Orsino make, and concludes,

> O time, thou must untangle this, not I!
> It is too hard a knot for me to untie!

Purpose

Viola, who is the only one in the play that knows the true situation, here becomes aware of the full round of the circle of lovers. She discovers that the disguise, which she thought would be of help, is in fact the cause of the complications; she cannot disclose herself as a proper object of Orsino's attention, nor can she reveal herself as an improper object of Olivia's love.

Notes

STRUCTURE
For four scenes in a row the love story has been presented, to the virtual exclusion of the comic. In Act I, Scene 4, we discover that Viola loves Orsino. In Scene 5, after a comic opening, we watch Olivia falling in love. Then, in Act II, Scene 1, we grasp the significance of Sebastian's arrival. And now we see Viola made aware that Olivia mistakenly loves her. The complicated opposition between appearance and reality, the difficulties that arise with the assumption of a role, are thus brought home to us by the consequences of Viola's disguise.

VIOLA'S REACTION TO THE RING
It is interesting to note that Viola does not contradict Malvolio when he says Cesario left the ring with Olivia. It is only after he goes that she says, "I left no ring with her," and ponders what it means. Critics have wondered why this is so. The best supposition seems to be that, knowing Malvolio's statement to be false, but recognizing that Malvolio believes it, the falsehood is not his but Olivia's. Viola senses there must be a purpose in the message unknown to the messenger. She consequently would not challenge the statement: first, because she had not yet probed its meaning; second, because she would not betray one of her own sex to a subordinate. A few actresses have spoken the lines as though in bewildered questioning: "She took the ring from?" But most seem to feel that it suits Viola better to make the statement a direct one.

Although Olivia had called Cesario a "peevish messenger," the statement that he "peevishly threw" the ring at her is entirely Malvolio's invention. Malvolio (as is further shown later, when he pictures himself as husband to Olivia), has a habit of building imaginary scenes in great detail.

ACT II · SCENE 3

Summary
This lengthy scene returns to the subplot, preparing us for the ridicule Malvolio will suffer later on. Sir Toby and Sir Andrew are together late at night, drinking boisterously. Sir Toby explains to his foolish friend his philosophy of life, which primarily consists of drinking and eating. The Clown comes to join them, and is congratulated by Sir Andrew on his "gracious fooling" during the past night. Both drunkards clamor for a song, and on being urged to sing a love song, not

a song of good life, the Clown sings, "O Mistress mine, where are you roaming?" His companions congratulate him on his sweet voice, and Sir Toby asks for a catch (a kind of round) that will "make the Welkin dance," or bring the house down. Sir Andrew proposes "Thou Knave," and after quibbling on the title of the song, all three sing loudly.

Maria comes in, complaining of the noise, adding that Malvolio is on the way to throw the trio out on orders from Olivia. Sir Toby pokes drunken fun at her threat, calling on his rights as Olivia's relative.

At this point, Malvolio enters. Angry and puffed up with self-importance, he pompously scolds the noise-makers, accusing them of empty-headedness, ill-breeding and shamelessness. Sir Toby rouses him to a white heat of anger with his frank request to shut up and leave. Malvolio informs him that Olivia will have none of his unruly conduct and that he may be forced to leave the house, unless he can stop his evil ways.

Sir Toby and the Clown, taking up Malvolio's last word, sing a song in comic dialogue, with Malvolio standing by helplessly. Sir Toby then defies Malvolio, "art any more than a steward," and laughs at his virtuous dislike of "cakes and ale" (carousing). Malvolio retreats, rebuking Maria for serving wine and flouting Olivia's wishes. He threatens to let Olivia hear of it.

Sir Andrew proposes to humiliate Malvolio by challenging him to a duel and then failing to turn up. Sir Toby agrees to the idea, but Maria has a better one. She asks Sir Toby to break off for the night out of consideration for Olivia, who is upset by the Duke's messenger. She proposes to deal with Malvolio herself, and really humiliate him. Asked by Sir Toby to let them in on what she is planning, she speaks of Malvolio as something of a Puritan, a time server, affected ass, and full of boundless self-conceit. She plans to attack him on that weak spot, to write love letters in Olivia's hand, praising Malvolio without giving his name, but in which he will "find himself most feelingly personated." Sir Toby guesses the drift of Maria's trick, and agrees with enthusiasm. Maria is sure that her "physic will work with him," and promises to plant the letters, with Sir Toby, Sir Andrew and the clown watching the steward from a hiding place. She is bid an affectionate goodnight by Sir Toby who says that she adores him. Sir Toby asks Sir Andrew to send for some more money, and assures him that his wooing of Olivia will bear eventual success. The two adjourn to drink some more sack before going to bed.

Purposes

1. The excesses of pompous self-love on the one hand and of boisterous revelry on the other are here contrasted. At the same time, Malvolio's affectation sheds light on the characters of Orsino and Olivia, who on their level have also been wrapped in self-centered affectation.

2. This scene does not contribute anything to the major plot. However, it does provide comic relief from the romantic developments, and it allows some time for the various love-relationships to ripen.

3. It prepares us for Malvolio's humiliation.

Notes

THE PURITAN AND THE ROISTERERS

Sir Toby states the contrast between the roisterers and the Puritan in his question to Malvolio which has become famous: "Dost thou think, because thou art virtuous, there shall be no more cakes and ale?"

Our sympathies may be with the pleasure-seekers, as opposed to the censorious Malvolio; but Shakespeare does not fail to show us that both extremes are antisocial.

A drinking scene of tipsy jokes and song always seems to go well on the stage. This is one of the first such scenes in English comedy; it has had a long trail of followers on the stages of two continents, providing laughter through the spectacle of boozy incontinence and incoherence.

Maria follows her reference to Malvolio as a Puritan with an immediate retraction. The Puritans were opposed to many indulgences, especially to the pleasures of the theater; but they were also a very strong segment of the English populace, which in half a century was able to overthrow the king. It was wise of Shakespeare to have the foppish and foolish Sir Andrew declare that if he thought Malvolio were a Puritan, he would "beat him like a dog." To be disliked by Sir Andrew is a wise man's praise; Sir Andrew himself is every bit as ludicrous a figure as Malvolio, with fewer redeeming features.

FESTE

In his previous appearance, the Clown was put down by Maria, Olivia and Malvolio. Here he displays his talents more fully. He readily joins in Sir Toby's fun in his ringing dialogue with him. He shows his skill in talking pure and amusing nonsense in invented names: Pigrogromitus, the Vapians, Queubus, impeticos, gratillity; and in his talk about "Malvolio's nose is no whipstock . . . the Myrmidons are no bottle-ale houses." He shows himself to be a lover of music. He says nothing after Malvolio's parting threat, as he seems afraid to be turned out of the house.

It was part of his job to always be available for entertaining members of the household and guests. He fully expected to be paid for his efforts, and he routinely accepts money from the knights; but it is obvious that he genuinely enjoys carousing with Sir Toby and Sir Andrew, and when he is with them, he is in especially good form.

FESTE'S LOVE SONG

Feste's song, like most in Shakespeare's plays, has a relevance to the play and place in which it is sung. Among the revelers come these merry

40

love lyrics, suggesting the sense of freedom based on the acceptance of disillusion: "Youth's a stuff will not endure." The easy-going household of Olivia is thus balanced against the taut and restless formality of Orsino's court.

SIR TOBY

He is the chief life of the party. He leads Sir Andrew, making him stay up and drink, ridicules Malvolio and tells him to get out, and calls for wine in his presence; he tells Sir Andrew to send for more money and assures him he will do everything necessary to win Olivia for him. He sings snatches of songs and takes great delight in noise. He shows his fondness for Maria, calling her "Penthesilea" and a "beagle, truebred." His treatment of Sir Andrew is proof of his slippery morals; he is a good-natured rogue.

SIR ANDREW

He follows Sir Toby's lead in everything, showing his lack of spirit, wit and originality. He is pursuaded to stay up longer, gives the fool money and is tricked into sending for more money to continue his suit of Olivia, without suspecting Sir Toby's real purpose. He proposes to challenge Malvolio to a duel and then walk out, a harmless plan in accord with his cowardice and lack of inventiveness.

MARIA

With Sir Toby, she is to play a major part in the fooling of Malvolio. She is disgusted at the noise and drinking, but shows herself to be a good sport, siding against Malvolio. She is fond of laughter and amusement, though not of brawling. She shows her intelligence in thinking up the plan to fool Malvolio. She "adores" Sir Toby for his humor and life, as he tells us.

MALVOLIO

This scene shows his pompous, self-important, peevish and joyless character perfectly. His speech sounds as if he were addressing a group of criminals in a court. He talks pompously, "have you no wit, manners, nor honesty . . . Is there no respect of place, person or time in you? . . . Sir Toby, I must be round with you." He shows his contempt for the others, treating them like inferiors or children.

ACT II · SCENE 4

Summary

After a scene of comedy and merriment, we are returned to the sentiment and poetry of the Duke's court. The music-loving Orsino is asking for a sad song he had heard the previous night to relieve his soul, still love-sick and yearning for Olivia. On being informed that the singer,

Feste, is not present, he sends for him and has the tune played in the meantime. His melancholy mood makes him wish to share his feeling with his page Cesario-Viola. He asks her to remember him as a true lover, if ever she should love, and asks how she likes the tune. Viola replies that it seems like the spirit of love itself. She is commended by the Duke for her answer and he adds that she must surely have known love. Without giving herself away, Viola states that the one she loves is like the Duke in looks and years. The Duke advises her to love a woman younger than herself; men's affections, in spite of self-praise, are more changing and inconstant than a woman's love. Viola agrees, and the Duke continues his advice that Cesario should choose a younger woman, or else love will die too soon; once a woman's beauty is ripe, it dies, like a rose. Viola laments the fate of women, "to die, even when they to perfection grow," implying her own fruitless love, which she must stifle.

Feste enters: the Duke asks for his song and asks Cesario to mark its simple truth or "silly sooth" of feeling. Feste sings the dirge "Come away, come away, death," refusing money for his pains, as singing is a pleasure to him. He leaves, first wishing the Duke the protection of Saturn, the god of melancholy temper. He jests on Orsino's inconstancy, comparing him to an opal. All retire except Viola. Orsino tells her to go again to Olivia and plead his great love, which makes him despise all wealth and rank. Viola objects that Olivia cannot love him. The Duke insists "I cannot be so answered." Viola wishing, but not daring, to tell him of her love, tells him he must accept Olivia's refusal. Orsino, somewhat boastingly, extols his own love; no woman can love so fully and insatiably. Woman's love is mere appetite; his is boundless like the sea. Viola persists, "Ay, but I know," and, prompted by the Duke, tells of the love a woman may bear a man, giving as an instance, that of "a daughter of her father" who loved a man, as she might love the Duke were she a woman. The Duke inquires as to the history of the girl. Viola states that it was a "blank"; she bore her love in silence, and pined away in grief:

> *Viola.* My father had a daughter loved a man,
> As it might be, perhaps, were I a woman,
> I should your lordship.
> *Orsino.*   And what's her history?
> *Viola.* A blank, my lord, She never told her love,
> But let concealment, like a worm i' the bud,
> Feed on her damask cheek. She pined in thought,
> And with a green and yellow melancholy
> She sat like Patience on a monument,
> Smiling at grief.

Men's love compared to hers is mere show. To the Duke's question, as to whether her sister died of her love, she replies that she is all that is left of her father's daughters and brothers. She breaks off hastily to return to the Duke's message to Olivia. The Duke gives her a jewel and bids her to tell Olivia that his love cannot wait or be refused.

Purposes

1. It maintains suspense by showing the dramatic irony of Viola's situation, almost to the point of revealing her love to the Duke.

2. It demonstrates Orsino's growing love-melancholy.

3. It contains beautiful poetry and song, to contrast with the comedy of the subplot.

4. It allows time for the gulling subplot to get under way.

5. The contrast between Orsino's protestations and the facts now becomes obvious. He contradicts himself by saying that he is constant in his love and then declaring that men are fickle in their fancies. This is emphasized in Feste's estimate of the Duke and pressed home by Viola's quiet presentation of a woman's deeper love. The Duke has Feste sing again the song of a man who has died of love; the very notion of it pleases him. All this prepares us for the time when we must accept as natural the Duke's falling out of love with Olivia and into a true love with Viola.

Notes

When Orsino asks Viola, "Died thy sister of her love, my boy?" she answers, in words we understand but the Duke does not, "I am all the daughters of my father's house." She adds, believing her brother drowned (but thereby reminding us he is alive nearby), "and all the brothers too."

SIGNIFICANCE OF COLORS

The colors of Viola's "melancholy" are significant, for colors then had definite associations. Green signified youth, and hope, and romance. Yellow (not gold) was linked with jealousy, inconstancy, treachery. In the play, of course, the colors have their milder connotations. Thus Viola may be indicating her hopefulness (tinged with a slight jealousy) that Orsino will prove inconstant in his present attachment, which he fondly calls love, and somehow become constant in true love to herself.

ORSINO'S ADVICE TO HIS PAGE

Orsino's advice to his page, that the woman should always "take an elder than herself," is assumed by some critics (including Coleridge) to be a personal reflection by the playwright, who had married a woman almost eight years his senior. However, we have no direct information — except that William made frequent and long visits to London, away from his wife, Anne — that the Shakespeares' marriage was an unhappy one.

SONG

There are suggestions in the dialogue here — as Orsino says to Cesario, "Come, but one verse," reenforced by Viola's mention (Act I, Scene 2) of her ability to sing — that the song in this scene was originally sung by Cesario, and was later, for reasons that can only be guessed, transferred to Feste.

Orsino desires a simple song, a plain song; the one Feste sings is a highly finished art song. But in asking for it, Orsino stresses the sense of belonging to a continuing fellowship:

> The spinsters and the knitters in the sun
> And the free maids that weave their thread with bones
> Do use to chant it. It is silly sooth,
> And dallies with the innocence of love
> Like the old age.

("Silly sooth" means *simple truth*.) C.L. Barber is deeply impressed by the prosody here: "The wonderful line about the free maids, which throws such firm stress on 'free' by the delayed accent, and then slows up in strong, regular monosyllables, crystallizes the play's central feeling for freedom in heritage and community."

EFFECT OF THE DISGUISE

As with Rosalind in *As You Like It*, the mood evoked by a male actor playing a woman disguised as a man is usually one of gaiety, of good fun and laughter. In the present scene, the conversation between Orsino and the disguised Viola arouses a very different feeling, one of sympathy and tender affection.

VIOLA

Although the passive lover whom Cesario pictures as his sister "never told her love," the active Viola manages to tell hers, and then moves on: "Sir, shall I to this lady?" Loving Orsino, she still will carry his message to Olivia.

ACT II · SCENE 5

Summary

The subplot reaches a climax in this scene. Sir Toby, Sir Andrew and Fabian come in filled with anticipation of the tricking of Malvolio. Fabian, a servant of Olivia, reveals his grudge against Malvolio who made him lose Olivia's favor as a result of a bear-baiting incident. Maria enters and hurries the three into the shrubbery, as Malvolio is coming along the walk, She remarks on his ridiculous behavior during the past half-hour, practising with his shadow. She throws the letter on the ground which is to make him a "contemplative idiot."

Malvolio comes onto the empty scene, watched by three men in hiding. He is talking to himself of the fancy which Olivia has for him, according to what Maria has told him. He thinks that she has more than respect for him. He falls to imagining himself Count Malvolio, raised from his steward's position, married to Olivia for three months and giving directions to his servants. He imagines himself treating Sir Toby with familiar condescension and taking him to task for his drinking and association with Sir Andrew. The three listeners in their hiding place, find it difficult to keep each other from jumping out and stopping or beating him.

Malvolio finds the letter and reads it in rapture. He takes it for Olivia's letter, "in contempt of question," and recognizes the hint at his name in the letters (M O A I). Solving the riddle of these letters, Malvolio proceeds to the prose part of the epistle. He is asked in it not to be afraid of greatness, but to rise joyously to the great situation due his excellence. He is instructed to be severe to a kinsman, meaning Sir Toby, to be surly towards the servants, to talk gravely of affairs of state, to be eccentric in behavior, wear yellow stockings and cross-garters. The letter is signed "The Fortune-Unhappy," who would wish to change places with Malvolio so that she could serve him. The effect of the letter is as desired. Malvolio determines to do all he is asked, he remembers that Olivia did admire his yellow stockings and cross-garters. He comes to the postscript, which asks him to smile in his mistress' presence, and leaves, vowing that he will smile and do all that is asked.

Sir Toby swears he could marry Maria for the perfect trick she has performed with the letter, and be content with another such jest in place of a dowry. Maria returns and is offered marriage by Sir Toby. She asks them to go to see Malvolio's behavior before Olivia, dressed in cross-garters and yellow stockings and smiling, all equally detested by Olivia in her present melancholy mood. Sir Toby enthusiastically cries that he will follow Maria to the gates of Tartar or hell itself.

Purpose

This scene is primarily concerned with the trick to be played upon Malvolio, paving the way for his ultimate humiliation. At the same time, Malvolio's fancy that he has become master of the house, confirmed in his mind by Maria's letter, parodies, on its comic level, the sentimental affectations of Orsino and Olivia. We are, moreover, subtly reminded that Olivia is moving out of her self-assigned role of the loving mourner; for when Maria describes her as "addicted to a melancholy" we are aware — as Maria and the rest of the household are not — that Olivia's mood has been quite changed by her newfound love for Cesario.

Notes

Observe that Malvolio has been fancying himself married to Olivia *before* he discovers Maria's letter. Her device thus seems to him to promise that his dream is coming true.

BEAR-BAITING

Bear-baiting, which could be seen in London in Shakespeare's time every Wednesday and Sunday, was a popular entertainment. A bear was tied to a pole in a pit, then four or five mastiffs were set upon him. Usually, the surviving dogs were pulled away before they killed the bear. Having Malvolio oppose the sport again links him with the Puritans, who were strongly against it, although, as Macaulay said, "not because it gave pain to the bear, but because it gave pleasure to the spectators." Malvolio, as Sir Toby sees him, is an arrant spoilsport.

"METTLE OF INDIA"

Sir Toby (in the First Folio), on seeing Maria, cries: "Here comes the little villain. How now, my mettle of India?" Shakespeare keeps us constantly in mind of Maria's small stature; she is a minx, from whom the pranks come more fittingly than they would from a woman of more imposing stature. The word *mettle*, however, has worried the editors. A number of them have changed it to *nettle*, stating that the "nettle of India" has a sweet-smelling flower — and a tormenting sting. More recently, however, editors have used the phrase *metal of India*, meaning fine gold.

M, O, A, I

The initials *M, O, A, I*, which Malvolio twists to suggest his name, are a form of riddle, or cypher, current at the time. The *Book of Merry Riddles* (1629) contains a typical rhyme:

> M and J made great moan
> When C on C was let alone.

The initials stand for Mary and John, Christ on a Cross.

M, O, A, I, one editor suggests, may stand for *My Own Adored Idol*. Leslie Hotson thinks Shakespeare more subtle still, and, by using Latin words: *Mare, Orbis, Aer, Ignis*, Hotson connects the letters with the four elements — water, earth, air, and fire. These were considered the basic components of all matter, and the physiology of the time could properly begin the line that ends, "doth sway my life." This is a subtlety, however, that seems beyond the grasp of Shakespeare's audience.

"FABIAN"

Fabian — though used by Bernard Shaw and the Fabian Society to mean one that moved slowly, one that employed delaying tactics — was, in Elizabethan days, a general nickname for a reveller, "a flaunting fabian."

YELLOW STOCKINGS

Yellow stockings were worn especially by the young gallants of the time. *Peg a Ramsay*, to which Sir Toby (Act III, Scene 3) likens Malvolio, is the song of a married man longing for the freedom of his bachelor days. Its refrain is:

> Give me my yellow hose again,
> Give me my yellow hose.

The idea seems to be that grave Malvolio is to dress like a giddy and frivolous lad.

USE OF "JOVE"

Malvolio twice refers to the Roman god Jove, "Jove, I thank thee." Such an exclamation comes oddly from the mouth of this earnest and strait-laced Christian. It has therefore been suggested that he naturally cried, in his great (and greatly mistaken) joy, "God, I thank thee!", but that the word was altered when King James I issued his stern statute against profanity.

MALVOLIO'S WATCH

Picturing himself the lord of the house, Malvolio says, "I frown the while, and perhaps wind up my watch, or play with my — some rich jewel." Apparently he is about to say "my chain," but then breaks off, with the recognition that he would no longer be wearing the steward's chain of office, but the master's colorful gems. The mention of a watch suggests great wealth, or elaborate ostentation. Of this line, Samuel Johnson remarked, "In our author's time watches were very uncommon. When Guy Fawkes was taken, it was urged as a circumstance of suspicion that a watch was found upon him."

ASIDES

There are two types of aside in the theater. The most frequent is that in which a character says something that only the audience is intended to hear. Such are the remarks of Sir Toby and Viola in the next scene, when he says he'll ride Sir Andrew's horse, and when she is on the brink of revealing her true sex. Similar asides end Scenes 4 and 5 of Act I. When extended, such an aside is called a soliloquy. There are a number of notable soliloquies in *Hamlet*; here, there are only Viola's at the end of Act II, Scene 2, and Sebastian's that opens Act IV, Scene 3. The second type of aside is the whisper of one character to another; it is supposedly not heard by other characters onstage. This type of aside runs through this scene, as Malvolio reads and comments on the letter, unaware of the three that gleefully whisper and watch.

THE SOPHY — DATING THE PLAY

When Malvolio goes out after reading the letter, Fabian declares, "I will not give my part of this sport for a pension of thousands to be paid from the Sophy." This contemporary allusion may help set the date of *Twelfth Night*. In 1597 Sir Anthony Shirley and his brothers Robert and Thomas set out on a mission to the Sophy (Shah) of Persia. Sir Anthony, suspected of disloyalty, never returned; but the others came back in September, 1600. Sir Robert boasted of the Sophy's many gifts, and lived in London in great splendor. An account of the journey, quickly printed, was as quickly suppressed (October 2) by order of the Council, and all copies were seized and burned.

FABIAN
When Maria plans to have Toby and Andrew hide to watch Malvolio, she says (Act II, Scene 3, 189) "Let the fool make a third." Instead, we find Fabian, here introduced into the play. Later, Fabian explains the mischief to Olivia; he can do this more acceptably than the others, because he is less involved.

SYMPATHY FOR MALVOLIO
It has been suggested that Malvolio, a man of principle though wholly lacking in humor, casts a shadow of Shakespeare's coming tragic period over the gaiety of *Twelfth Night*. Especially in Act III, Scene 4, when the steward is confined in the dark room, the Romantics turned in sympathy toward the excessively punished Malvolio. But Charles Lamb, with regard to this scene at least, feels a delight even in the steward's false expectancy and hollow joy, "You rather admired than pitied the lunacy while it lasted; you felt that an hour of such mistake was worth an age with the eyes open . . . The man seemed to tread upon air, to taste manna, to walk with his head in the clouds, to mate Hyperion." In this way, the audience takes double delight: in the trickery of the three that watch the snare close, and in the ecstatic anticipation of the deluded victim.

ACT III · SCENE 1

Summary
Viola has come to Olivia's garden on her second mission from the Duke. She meets the Clown and she asks whether he lives by his labor and music. Feste enters upon a series of bantering replies, punning and playing upon Viola's words. Asked whether he is Olivia's fool, he answers that Olivia has no fool as she is unmarried. He flatters Viola on her wisdom and, in return, is given money. The fool wishes her a beard and goes to tell Olivia of Viola's presence. While waiting, Viola thinks about the wit of fools like Feste. Sir Toby and Sir Andrew, both surprisingly sober, enter. The latter addresses Viola in French; Sir Toby asks her to go inside. Olivia and Maria enter the garden and Viola assumes her courtier role, addressing Olivia in high-flown terms which are noted by Sir Andrew for future use. Olivia dismisses all except Viola and asks for her hand and name. Viola declares herself Olivia's servant, on the grounds that she is Orsino's servant and the Duke is Olivia's. Olivia replies that she does not wish to think of Orsino. She then explains the sending of the ring after Viola, apologizing for misusing

herself, Malvolio and Viola. She excuses herself, saying that her great love for Viola has made her override the bounds of convention and courtesy, and asks Viola to speak, now that she knows fully of her love. Viola pities Olivia, who takes it for a degree of love. Viola denies it, since one often pities an enemy. Olivia grows proud and haughty, saying that it would be better to yield to the lion, Orsino, than the inferior wolf, his page. She decides to cut short her talk with Viola, promises that she will cease pursuing her, and wishes her luck. Asked by Viola if there is any message to the Duke, Olivia bids her to stay and give her opinion of her. Viola replies, "you do think you are not what you are," implying Olivia's ignorance that she is in love with a woman. Olivia replies that she thinks Viola is not what she seems. Viola replies, "I am not what I am," and Olivia wishes she were different and in love with her. To Viola's answer, "now I am your fool," Olivia comments on her beauty even in anger and contempt, and passionately confesses her full love for Viola. Viola can only say in turn that she loves no woman and never will, then leaves. Olivia asks her to return, for perhaps she may yet accept Orsino's love.

Purposes

1. The discussion of the double meanings of words suggests the dual role played by Viola, and the dual aspects of Olivia — as melancholy mourner and as ardent wooer. Feste's statement that folly "shines everywhere" comes midway in the play, and it refers to the events occurring both before and after it.

2. The love of Olivia for Cesario is now fully stated. First Olivia recognized her love; then Viola discerned it; now Olivia tells it to the page.

3. This scene, by its quiet tone and lack of action, supplies dramatic relief from the comic scene which precedes it.

Notes

WOMEN WOOING

It is understandable that Olivia should take the initiative toward Cesario. It would be presumption on the part of a page to woo a lady — especially as the page is emissary of his master's love. In the lady, it is a gracious unbending — made inappropriate only by the fact, unknown to Olivia, that the page is of her own sex. Leslie Hotson, however, suggests that Shakespeare has the woman woo because it is leap year (1600).

"OUT OF MY ELEMENT" — DATING THE PLAY

On leaving to report Cesario's arrival, Feste tells the page that what he wants is none of the Fool's business, "Who are you and what you would are out of my welkin; I might say 'element,' but the word is overworn." The phrase "out of my element" is similarly mocked in Dekker's *Satiromastix* ("Satire's Scourge"), a play written in 1601, so *Twelfth Night* might be of a later date than some conjecture.

LANGUAGE

In the brief exchange between the knights and the page, two details may be noted. We have learned of Sir Andrew's ignorance of French; here, however, he delivers a salutation in the proper form. He catches the meaning of the last word of Viola's answer; it is *serviteur*, pronounced almost the same in both languages, but he answers her in English. Sir Toby, on the other hand, seeks to ridicule the page with pompously polite if not pedantic phrases — "Taste your legs, sir" (another instance of food imagery), meaning "Go in"; but Viola gives him as good as she gets.

OLIVIA'S CONFUSION

The striking of the clock, while Olivia is telling her love to Cesario, brings her back to reality:

> The clock upbraids me with the waste of time.
> Be not afraid, good youth, I will not have you.

Some editors, remarking that Olivia can hardly reject the youth before he has proposed, emend *have* to *harm*, or suggest that Olivia, in her emotion, breaks off with her sentence incomplete. However, in the next line she looks wryly ahead:

> And yet, when wit and youth is come to harvest,
> Your wife is like to reap a proper man.

Here again, any amusement we may feel at the misunderstanding caused by Viola's masquerade is tinged with sympathy for the misled Olivia.

Viola is constantly alert, and ready with fit words. It is perhaps because she alone can match Feste jest for jest that she alone receives from him an ungracious word, "I do not care for you." Olivia recognizes Cesario's awareness; she says, "To one of your receiving Enough is shown . . . So let me hear you speak." And Viola responds, "I pity you." Olivia, of course, continues to misunderstand. The scene piles one humorous situation upon another: a woman does the wooing, and the one she woos is not a man — yet the deeper human qualities appeal to us more than the comic.

ACT III · SCENE 2

Summary

A second subplot is prepared in this scene. Sir Andrew tells Sir Toby and Fabian about his intention to leave Olivia's house. Pressed for the reason, he states that he has seen Viola (Cesario) shown more favors and consideration by Olivia than she ever showed him. Sir Toby and Fabian, smelling the occasion for a trick on him, inform Sir Andrew that Olivia's conduct is proof of her affection for him. Fabian convinces Sir Andrew that Olivia wished to awaken his "dormouse valour" by jealousy of Viola. Sir Andrew should have "banged the youth into dumbness" with some clever remarks. The only chance to retrieve his lady's favor lies in a stroke of intrigue or of valor. Sir Andrew boasts that valor is more to his taste than "policy" or intrigue. Sir Toby persuades him to produce a challenge, to be written "in a martial hand," curt and brief, with taunts, and full of wit and invention. Sir Andrew goes to write the letter. Fabian calls him a "dear manakin to you, Sir Toby"; the latter replies that he has been dear to Sir Andrew, to the tune of 2000 ducats. He agrees not to deliver Sir Andrew's letter, but to give the challenge by word of mouth. They anticipate great fun in forcing the cowardly knight and the Duke's gentle page to a duel. Maria joins them and tells them to hurry to see Malvolio. He has turned "heathen, a very renegado," parading in yellow stockings and cross-garters, smiling and doing all as instructed in the letter.

Purposes

1. It presents the subplot of Sir Toby and Fabian against Sir Andrew and Viola.

2. It reveals that Olivia's love for Viola is even suspected by Sir Toby.

3. It shows Sir Toby's relationship with Sir Andrew in its true light.

4. It works up to the crisis of the trick practised on Malvolio.

Notes

CONTEMPORARY ALLUSIONS

The ninety lines of this scene contain four allusions to contemporary persons or events:

(1) Fabian tells Sir Andrew: ". . . you are now sailed into the north of my lady's opinion, where you will hang like an icicle on a Dutchman's beard unless you do redeem it by some laudable attempt either of valor or of policy." The Dutchman Barentz had just discovered Novaya Zembla, a permanently ice-covered island in the Arctic Ocean; an account of the voyage was registered in the books of the Stationer's Company in 1598.

(2) Sir Andrew responds to Fabian: "An't be any way, it must be with valor, for policy I hate. I had as lief be a Brownist as a politician." The Brownists were an especially independent and strict sect of Puritans, constantly satirized toward the end of the sixteenth century. The founder of the sect, Robert Brown, after returning to the Church of England, grew insolent and violent, and was sent to Northampton jail about 1590. He boasted that he had been confined in thirty-two different prisons.

(3) Toby tells Sir Andrew to fill his challenge to Cesario with as many martial lies as will lie on the paper, "although the sheet were big enough for the bed of Ware in England . . ." The bed survives to the present day; it stands seven feet six inches high, and is ten feet nine inches in length and breadth. The earliest reference we have to the bed was made by Prince Ludwig of Anhalt-Köthen, on his visit to England in 1596. The Prince said that four couples could comfortably rest in it. The bed was for many years at *The Saracen's Head* tavern in Ware, some twenty-three miles north of London. In 1864 it was sold at an auction for a hundred guineas, and is now, according to the *Oxford Companion to English Literature*, in the Victoria and Albert Museum in London.

(4) Maria, speaking of Malvolio, says, "He does smile his face into more lines than is in the new map with the augmentation of the Indies." There is some dispute as to which map this was; but most agree that it was drawn by, or according to the specifications of, Edward Wright, perhaps under the supervision of the travel writer Richard Hakluyt, and published in 1600. It is criss-crossed with rhumb-lines and, incidentally, includes the newfound island of Novaya Zembla, referred to in (1) above.

Shakespeare makes several references to the liver as the seat of courage; a bloodless liver marked a coward. In *Macbeth* (Act I, Scene 3, 15) Macbeth rebukes the "lily-livered boy." In *The Merchant of Venice* (Act III, Scene 2, 86) Bassanio speaks of "livers white as milk." Here, Sir Toby, speaking of his gull, Sir Andrew, builds a more vivid image, "If he were opened and you find so much blood in his liver as will clog the foot of a flea, I'll eat the rest of the anatomy."

SIR TOBY
He shows his zest for practical jokes in arranging for the duel between Sir Andrew and Viola. His knowledge of Sir Andrew is displayed by feeding on his vanity and by his intention not to give his letter to Viola, since it will probably be too foolish to frighten her. He is unscrupulous in using Sir Andrew whom he already cheated for 2000 ducats. He affectionately speaks of Maria as the "youngest wren of mine."

FABIAN
He is ready to enter the spirit of the game, and follows up Sir Toby cleverly by appealing to the knight's vanity. He does not think that Sir Toby will carry the fooling into actual practice by giving the letter to Viola.

SIR ANDREW
His stupidity, vanity and weak will are displayed. He falls for Sir Toby's and Fabian's explanation of Olivia's conduct to Viola, changes his mind under Sir Toby's influence, and is ready to challenge Viola in spite of his cowardice.

ACT III · SCENE 3

Summary

From the fast-increasing complications of events in Olivia's house and at the Duke's palace, this scene takes us back to Sebastian, who, since his appearance in Act II, Scene 1, has made his way to the capital of Illyria. Unexpectedly, he meets his friend Antonio who has secretly followed him. Sebastian has just scolded Antonio; the latter excuses himself, saying that he was driven on by his love of Sebastian and fear that he might have a hard time in Illyria as a stranger. Sebastian thanks him for his devotion, wishing he could reward him. He proposes to see the town's sights, but Antonio begs to be excused from accompanying him. To explain, he says that he was once involved in a sea battle against the Duke's ships, and now is afraid of being recognized. To Sebastian's question as to whether he killed many of the Duke's men, he replies that his crime was not "of such a bloody nature," though there was occasion for it, but that he was the only one of his town not to make up for the goods they took from Orsino's ships. He decides to stay at the Elephant, an inn on the outskirts of the town, to wait for Sebastian. He gives his purse to Sebastian, in case he should wish to buy something. They agree to meet at the inn in an hour.

Purposes

1. It reintroduces Sebastian to the story and prepares us for further complications of the main plot by reminding us of Sebastian's resemblance to Viola.

2. It tells of Antonio's fear of the Duke's court and prepares us for his later arrest.

Notes

After the duel with Viola has been planned, it is an apt moment to remind us that Viola has a twin brother. We are thus prepared to have the tables turned upon the tricksters. Everything is now plotted by the characters and prepared by the author; we have only to see the results of the machinations and misunderstandings.

ANTONIO

He shows great courage and generous devotion to Sebastian in coming into the town of his enemies. His recklessness is to cost him dearly later. He shows generosity in giving his purse to his friend.

SEBASTIAN

He gives further proof of his good nature by scolding Antonio for following him into danger, and by his wish to repay him for his kindness. He has no definite course of action, but desires to while away some time, seeing the town and finding out about it.

ACT III · SCENE 4

Summary
This is the longest scene in the play. It contains a generous measure of humor and comedy, and brings the subplots of Malvolio's gulling and of the duel to a head.

Olivia is excitedly waiting for Viola to respond to her summons. She has decided to give her a feast in order to win her love. She asks Maria for Malvolio, and is told that he is coming "in very strange manner," smiling as if he were mad. Olivia sends Maria to get him, while comparing her own melancholy with Malvolio's gay madness. Malvolio enters with Maria; he beams at Olivia and kisses her hand crying out, "Sweet Lady, ho, ho." Taken aback, Olivia asks the reason for his smiles, which do not fit with the solemn occasion on which she has sent for him. Malvolio replies that he could be sad, for his cross-garters hurt his legs, but, since it is her wish, he aims to please her with them. To her astonished question as to what is the matter with him, he cheerfully replies, "not black in my mind, though yellow in my legs," and alludes to the "sweet Roman hand of the letter." Olivia takes him to be ill; Malvolio quotes from the supposed letter, referring to the passages on his greatness, the yellow stockings, and cross-garters. His wild babbling and behavior convince her that he is suffering from "midsummer madness."

Viola is announced and Olivia hurries off, asking Maria to have Malvolio looked after by Sir Toby. Malvolio, left alone for a moment, soliloquizes on her order to have Sir Toby take care of him. He sees further evidence in this of the truth of the letter; Sir Toby is sent to be dealt with harshly by him. He quotes part of the letter's instructions and rejoices in his skill in catching Olivia, thanking God for his good fortune. In his self-deception, he takes Olivia's use of "fellow," instead of "Malvolio," for a good sign, and sees his hopes fully realized.

Maria returns with Sir Toby and Fabian, approaching Malvolio as if he were a madman, his hollow voice showing him to be possessed by the devil. Sir Toby wishes to deal gently with him so as not to provoke the devil in him, and addresses him like a child or half-wit. Malvolio replies to them in terms of haughty contempt, already imagining himself a count, and leaves, threatening to punish them for their insolence later. Sir Toby hits upon the idea of shutting him in a dark room like a lunatic, and carrying the joke as far as their pity and decency will allow.

While still debating their further treatment of Malvolio, the three schemers are joined by Sir Andrew. Fabian immediately senses "more matter for a May morning" of frolic and revelry. Sir Andrew shows them the challenge to Viola. Sir Toby reads the letter out in full, Fabian adding comments on the foolish writing with tongue-in-cheek. Maria informs them that Viola is with Olivia. Sir Andrew is sent off by Sir Toby to await Viola in the orchard and attack her with a series of great oaths. Sir Toby decides not to deliver the letter because its "excellent ignorant" nature would not frighten the page. Instead he will make up some horrible challenge to scare Viola out of her wits, so that the duelists will kill each other with looks, like basilisks (mythological creatures able to cause death by their look or breath).

The schemers leave, and Olivia enters with Viola. She admits that her passion for Viola has made her forget all dignity and self-restraint. Viola counters that Orsino's grief is just as strong. She is given a jewel with Olivia's picture and asked to come again the next day. Olivia leaves, assuring Viola she would even follow her to hell. Left all alone, Viola is joined by Sir Toby and Fabian. Sir Toby does his best to frighten her with his challenge. He warns her that her enemy, "bloody as the hunter" for unknown wrongs, is waiting at the orchard-end. Sir Andrew is pictured as strong, young, skillful and furious, a knight of the carpet, a "devil in private brawl" with three slain men to his credit and implacably bloodthirsty at the moment. Viola is bewildered; she is unaware of having offended any man, and decides to ask Olivia for an escort. She takes Sir Andrew for a habitual brawler, but Sir Toby assures her that Sir Andrew has good reason for the duel, and threatens to fight her, if she does not go to meet him. Viola, exasperated by his uncivil behavior, makes him go to find out why she is being challenged to the duel. While Sir Toby is away, she asks Fabian for the reason of the challenge. He also refuses to tell; instead he verbally paints a picture of Sir Andrew's valor and bloodiness and proposes to prevail upon him to drop the duel. Viola agrees, implying that she would rather be party to a marriage than a duel.

At this moment, Sir Toby returns, dragging the trembling Sir Andrew along with him. He terrifies the cowardly knight with a description of Viola's fierceness, calling her a "very devil" and a "firago." He tells him that he just had a bout with Viola, and that she is reputed to have been fencer to the Shah of Persia. Sir Andrew's only thought is to get away from his fearful opponent. He confesses that he would never have challenged Viola, had he known of her valor and fencing skill. Now, he wants to drop the challenge and offer Viola his gray horse, Capilet. Sir Toby pretends to make the offer to Viola, secretly resolving to keep Sir Andrew's horse for himself. He convinces Viola that there is no way out of the duel; Sir Andrew will not hurt her, but will only fight for the sake of his oath. Viola prays for help. Sir Toby assures the knight that Viola will not hurt him, and the duelists draw.

At this moment, Antonio enters unexpectedly. He mistakes Viola for Sebastian and offers to give satisfaction for any fault that she may have committed. Sir Toby draws his sword, but several officers of the law enter. Both duelists are glad to put up their swords, as dueling is unlawful. The officers recognize Antonio, whose presence has become known in the city and for whom a warrant has been sent out. Antonio pretends that he is the wrong man, but then decides to surrender to the law. As he is about to go with the police, he turns to Viola, telling her that his search for her had led to his arrest, but that he bears no ill feelings. He asks for his purse, apologizing that necessity forces him to do so. Viola, surprised at his strange request, offers to lend him some money in return for his kind interference in the duel and for his difficult position. She will give him half of what she has. Antonio accuses her of hard-heartedness for refusing him his purse in his present trouble. He is ready to recall the kind acts he has done for her. To his dismay, Viola denies knowing of them and having ever seen Antonio before; she eloquently attacks ingratitude as the worst vice of all. Antonio resists the attempts of the police to take him away and tells the bystanders that the youth, Viola (Sebastian), was rescued by him from death and treated kindly, because he thought that her outward beauty showed a fair soul. He bitterly denounces her for her ingratitude again, calling her Sebastian while he is hurried off by the officers who think he is mad.

His reference to Sebastian leaves Viola in a state of wild excitement. She is half-convinced that her brother is still alive and safe, for she suspects that her resemblance to him has caused Antonio to confuse her with Sebastian.

She leaves and Sir Toby and Fabian egg on Sir Andrew to follow her, convincing him of her dishonesty and cowardice. They advise him to use his fists not his sword, in order to keep within the law, and go after him to see the outcome of their trick.

Purposes

1. It presents the climax of the subplot centered on Malvolio.

2. It anticipates the final humiliation of Malvolio in the dark chamber.

3. It continues the plot evolved by Sir Toby and Fabian, centering on Sir Andrew's duel with Viola.

4. It anticipates the surprise ending by introducing another series of mistaken identities.

5. It contains a great deal of comedy, in Malvolio's appearance before Olivia, and in the farcical duel.

Notes

MADNESS

When Malvolio is first summoned, after Maria's words of his strange, insistently smiling behavior, Olivia reflects:

> I am as mad as he,
> If sad and merry madness equal be.

The words *mad* and *madness* occur more frequently in this play than in any other of Shakespeare's. And indeed, if madness be deviation from the norm, some taint of it stains almost every person in the play. It is with some logic that, in the next scene, the bewildered Sebastian cries, "Are all the people mad?"

THE CHALLENGE TO CESARIO

Even while trying to frighten Orsino's page with word of Sir Andrew's tigerish fierceness, Sir Toby cannot hide his contempt for the foolish fellow. He points out that Andrew is a carpet knight, that is, one dubbed, not on the field of honor, but kneeling indoors on a carpet, for other considerations than his valor, usually financial. Indeed, Sir Toby's remarks are almost as absurdly phrased as Sir Andrew's own challenge; it would frighten only an arrant coward — or a Cesario, a woman in disguise:

> Souls and bodies hath he divorced three, and his incensement
> at this moment is so implacable that satisfaction can be none
> but by pangs of death and sepulcher. Hob, nob, is his word,
> give't or take't.

MALVOLIO'S CONFUSION

Malvolio, bound by his self-love, is the most desperately entangled of all the characters. Olivia, though she speaks of her "sad madness," is sane enough to recognize it, and healthy enough to have broken through her melancholy to a more soundly directed love. But even when Malvolio preens himself on his new power, as prospective lord of the manor, he is even more firmly caught in his delusion. Shakespeare gives this mental condition a physical parallel, for Malvolio says, of the garter that binds his leg both below and above the knee, "This does make some obstruction in the blood." The obstruction in the blood is a parallel to 'he confusion in his mind.

The doting Malvolio thinks that he has won Olivia's heart; he sees everyone around as bowing to his will, for, "it is with me as the very true sonnet is, 'Please one, and please all.'" *Sonnet* was a term loosely used in Shakespeare's time and Malvolio is quoting a ballad which begins:

> The crow sits upon the wall,
> Please one and please all.

There is considerable talk, especially by Maria, to the effect that Malvolio is bewitched. Fabian joins her in the teasing. Sir Toby, of course, adds his wit. When he cautions Malvolio, "'Tis not for gravity to play at cherry-pit with Satan," he is referring to the children's game of tossing cherry pits into a hole; but possibly he is also alluding to the frequently mentioned witches (as in Thomas Nash's *Pierce Penniless*, 1592) with faces so wrinkled you could pitch cherry pits into the hollows.

THE "DUELS"

Productions frequently present an actual duel between Viola and Andrew, with each retreating as the other timidly extends his sword, before Antonio breaks in. There is no indication, in the dialogue or the stage directions, that this should take place, and there are two good reasons why it should not. First, such a duel, while it may amuse some in the audience, may also make Viola look foolish, and nowhere in the play does Shakespeare present her in such a light. Furthermore, as Cesario, she is not a coward; she shrinks from the conflict, but no more than a peaceable gentleman, conscious of having given no offense, would incline to do. (Accustomed as we are to stage bullies, we must not confuse gentleness with cowardice.) Her last words, before drawing her sword, are, "I do assure you, 'tis against my will." But she does draw. In the second place, Shakespeare has in this comedy left behind the horseplay and physical foolery of earlier comic scenes. The duel does not take place.

Later, when Sir Andrew strikes Sebastian, he returns the blow with interest, but before he and Sir Toby can begin to fight, Olivia interrupts. And in the final scene, although Andrew and Toby limp in, bloodied, the beating Sebastian gave them was delivered offstage.

EXORCISTS
Some editors find, in the words of witches and "finders of madmen," echoes of the several cases of Puritans and exorcists then in the public eye and ear. In particular, John Darrell, a Puritan preacher, in 1596 gained a reputation as a driver-out of evil spirits from those possessed. Some of those he cured later confessed that they were frauds, and Darrell was imprisoned for examination. A number of pamphlets on the question of exorcism were published between 1596 and 1602; one in 1600 records that, when the preachers asked for a Bible, the possessed children cried, "Reach them the bibble babble, bibble babble." Feste, in Act IV, Scene 2, pretending to be Sir Topas the curate, bids Malvolio, "Leave thy vain bibble-babble."

OLIVIA
Both Olivia and Viola are sad and subdued in this scene. Olivia is more hopelessly in love with Viola than before; she does not give up her pursuit. Her melancholy is in striking protest to the wild folly of the others in her house. She calls for Malvolio, because his "sad and civil" behavior goes well with her mood. Her condition makes her all the more disgusted with Malvolio's strange conduct, which she has already been prepared for by Maria. She has him looked after like a madman by Sir Toby, not suspecting that he is responsible (with Maria) for the state of Malvolio. In her interview with Viola she appears less excited than on previous occasions; she has become reconciled to humiliating her pride before Viola, and still persists, giving Viola a jewel with her picture on it. She carries her grief with a quieter dignity than before.

VIOLA
Her role in the scene is a difficult one. She is forced to continue her beloved Duke's suit to Olivia, and has to discourage Olivia's love for

her. Moreover, she is challenged to a duel for unknown reasons by Sir Andrew, and has to endure charges of ingratitude from another stranger, Antonio, without being able to defend herself convincingly. In each case she is prevented from solving her dilemma by revealing who she is. She makes the best of her situation, proving loyal in her duties to the Duke.

Sir Toby's communication of the challenge frightens her and she is stopped from seeking an escort from Olivia by Sir Toby's threat to draw his sword against her. She is equally afraid of fighting against a supposedly formidable enemy, unskilled in fencing as she is, and fears to reveal her female identity, which would destroy her hopes of staying on with the Duke. She decides to duel, assured that she will not be hurt, and is saved by Antonio. His intervention in the duel plunges her into further trouble, however. She is bewildered by his claims of her ingratitude and his insistence on his purse. She shows her generous nature in readily offering him half of her scanty wealth and in denouncing ingratitude as the worst of sins. After Antonio's removal by the police, she is filled with joy at the thought that he imagined her to be Sebastian, which proves that her brother must still be alive. She sees hope that she will see him again and that all her troubles will come to an end.

ACT IV · SCENE 1

Summary

The clown Feste has been sent to look for Viola. Meeting Sebastian before the Countess' house by chance, he naturally mistakes him for her and asks him to come inside. Sebastian is baffled and tells him to be off. He takes Feste's jesting replies for deliberate folly and angrily gives him some money, in place of "worse payment," should Feste continue to pester him. At this point Sir Andrew comes along followed by Sir Toby and Fabian and, seeing Sebastian, promptly pounces on him with the words "Now, sir, have I met you again? Here's for you." Sebastian retaliates with blows, thinking Sir Andrew is a madman, like the Clown. Sir Toby stops him and Sir Andrew threatens to have an action of battery brought against Sebastian, though he started the fight himself. Sebastian angrily asks Sir Toby to let go of his hand, and they both draw to fight. Olivia, fetched by Feste, enters in haste, tells Sir Toby to be off and apologizes to Sebastian. She asks him to enter the house and cool his rage by hearing of the pranks which Sir Toby has engaged in. Sebastian is hopelessly amazed, not knowing whether he is mad or dreaming all that has happened since he met the Clown. He asks his pleasant dream to continue, and willingly agrees to Olivia's request.

Purpose

Further misunderstanding begins to clear the way to the happy ending. Now Olivia, by error, corrects her earlier error, and courts a man. Sir Andrew is already paying the price of his foolishness, and Sir Toby is about to pay for his pranks.

Notes

Feste is the first of five characters that, here in quick succession, mistake Sebastian for Cesario. In this scene, Sebastian alone is not mistaken. But he is mystified.

LANGUAGE

When Sebastian gives generously to the Fool, Feste comments, rather cynically, "These wise men that give fools money get themselves a good report after fourteen years' purchase." Land in those days was valued at twelve times the annual rent; Feste is therefore saying that men overpay for the "good report" that gifts may bring them.

There have been several scholarly comments about Sebastian's calling Feste "foolish *Greek*." Some consider it an error for *geck*, a buffoon. But the elderly comedy *Ralph Roister Doister*, by Udall, has a character called Matthew Merygreek, and there are many contemporary references to the merry Greeks. A few scholars, however, suggest that *Greek* here is a term for a go-between, as Sebastian is being solicited by Feste to visit his mistress.

Although the passages just before and after are in prose (verse entering the scene with Olivia), some editors would have Sebastian beat Sir Andrew in meter. They therefore, to his line, "Why, there's for thee, and there, and there," add another "and there" — and another blow.

SEBASTIAN

He gives proof in this scene of his courage and quick temper. He lacks Viola's wit and sense of humor, is harsh in his talk to the Clown, and is quickly angered by Sir Andrew's sudden, cowardly attack. He meets a worthier opponent in Sir Toby, but challenges him to fight. He is quite ignorant of the stir his arrival causes in Olivia, suspecting nothing of the true state of her feelings towards him, her supposed Cesario. He, however, falls in readily with her wish to have him in her house, and is obviously taken with her charm and beauty from the first. This prepares for his quick falling in love with Olivia.

ACT IV · SCENE 2

Summary

The three chief schemers, Maria, Sir Toby and the Clown put the crowning indignity on Malvolio in this scene. They decide to carry out their intention of Act III, Scene 4, to truly drive him mad. The Clown is given a false beard and black gown by Maria, in order to assume the part of Sir Topas the curate, while Maria goes to fetch Sir Toby. Feste addresses Sir Toby imitating the solemn tone of a parson, crying, "What ho, I say peace in this prison." Malvolio, hearing that a curate is outside the dark room in which he has been shut up, asks the Clown in pathetic tones to see Olivia for his sake. Feste solemnly tells the devil to leave Malvolio (who will speak "nothing but of ladies"). Malvolio claims that great wrong has been done to him but that he is not mad. Feste torments him by telling him that the house is not dark, but that Malvolio's mental darkness makes it so. To Malvolio's answer to have his supposed madness put to the test, the Clown asks him the opinion of Pythagoras concerning wild fowl. Malvolio's answer is correct and his own opinion of Pythagoras also shows sanity, but the fool persists in treating him like a madman and pretends to leave. Sir Toby praises him for his part as curate and asks him to revert to his own voice, for he is now afraid that he has carried the joke too far (being already in disgrace with Olivia over the duel and attack on Sebastian). He leaves with Maria, while Feste returns to Malvolio. Singing a ditty, "Hey, Robin, jolly Robin, Tell me how thy lady does," he ignores Malvolio while singing, but listens in the end to Malvolio's plea to help him get writing materials and a light. Feste asks him how he happened to turn mad and to Malvolio's reply, "I am as well in my wits fool as thou art," Feste gets his own revenge on him by telling him he must be mad, since he is no better than a fool. Falling back into the role of Sir Topas, he tells him to rest his mad brain by sleeping and pretends to go. He finally promises to get what he is asked for when Malvolio offers him a reward. He goes, singing a farcical song about the devil and the Vice.

Purposes

1. It completes the subplot of Malvolio's humiliation.

2. It creates some sympathy for Malvolio who seems more than duly punished.

3. It mentions Olivia's displeasure at Sir Toby for his practical jokes.

4. It lets time elapse between Sebastian's coming to Olivia's house and his marriage to her.

Notes

FESTE AS THE CURATE

Feste is a shrewd Fool. He masks his frequent nonsense with pretense of learning, as in his greeting to Sir Toby, beginning with incorrect Latin:

> Bonos dies, Sir Toby. For, as the old hermit
> of Prague, that never saw pen and ink, very
> wittily said to a niece of King Gorboduc,
> "That that is is."

And occasionally he thrusts through the mists of foolery a flash of wisdom, as when denying that Malvolio's room is dark, he says in the

61

accents of the curate: "Madman, thou errest. I say, there is no darkness but ignorance."

ELIZABETHAN ATTITUDE TOWARD MADNESS

It should be kept in mind, in considering this scene, that the Elizabethan attitude toward madness differed greatly from ours. Confinement in a dark room, often in chains, was normal treatment. Some of the afflicted were exhibited in cages, and the public flocked to watch the antics at Bedlam (i.e., Bethlehem Hospital, incorporated in 1547 as a royal foundation for the reception of lunatics) as citizens today go to the zoo.

FIVE WITS

Feste asks Malvolio, "How fell you besides your five wits?" When Malvolio answers, "I am as well in my wits, fool, as thou art," Feste retorts, "Then you are mad indeed, to be no better in your wits than a fool." The "five wits" were the intellect, imagination, fantasy, judgment, and memory.

USE OF "JOVE"

When Sir Toby sees Feste in a curate's robe, he says, "Jove bless thee, Master parson." It may be that Toby is saying "Jove" in jest, but it is probable that the natural expression "God bless thee," which would have sprung to his lips, was altered because of the statute of James I against profanity.

SIR TOBY

He has carried his joke to the point of fearing Olivia's displeasure, which has already been aroused by his rude treatment of Sebastian. Hence, he tries to finish the baiting of Malvolio and gives no great show of his customary rough humor. He still enjoys Feste's playing the curate but asks him to look after the steward while he leaves with Maria.

MALVOLIO

This scene is his total downfall. He has been tormented beyond endurance, and his vanity and self-conceit have been shocked out of him. We feel that he has been punished sufficiently. Humility is his new keynote. He is still imposed upon by Feste's playing the curate, but he is still sane as his answers to Feste's questions show. He is willing to ask help even from the fool whom he has always despised. His cringing to Feste is somewhat disgusting, but his pitiful condition arouses sympathy. No word of revenge is breathed by him in this scene.

ACT IV . SCENE 3

Summary

Sebastian has been in Olivia's house only a short while, totally confused about the recent events leading to his entering her service. He assures himself that the world about him is real, that he is holding a real pearl given to him by Olivia, and that all is wonder, but not madness. He reveals, in his soliloquy, that he looked for Antonio at the Elephant, but heard that he had gone to seek him in the town. He would like to have his advice now, for the "accident and flood of fortune," which has suddenly overwhelmed him still seems too good to be true. He is forced to assume that either he or "the lady" is mad; yet her bearing and running of her house is not compatible with madness.

Olivia hurries in, interrupting Sebastian's misgivings on his fortune. She brings a priest along, and, excusing her haste, she asks Sebastian's hand in marriage, in order to appease her "most jealous and too doubt-ful soul." The marriage is to be kept secret until he chooses to have it made public. Sebastian agrees, swearing eternal faithfulness to her.

Purposes

1. Viola's predicament is now halfway resolved. She is free of Olivia; she now must bind Orsino.

2. It solves Olivia's (and the dramatist's) dilemma by bringing her together with Sebastian.

Notes

SEBASTIAN'S SOLILOQUY

Sebastian's soliloquy, his wonder at what is taking place, expresses the mood of the audience. And since we share his wonder, we more readily accept his resolve to move along with the events. He is, after all, a penniless young man in a strange country, approached with an honorable and loving proposal by an attractive and wealthy young lady.

SEBASTIAN'S ENGAGEMENT

The ceremony in the chapel is not a wedding, but a formal engagement in the presence of a witness, which in those days was equally as binding.

OLIVIA

Her confusion of Viola and Sebastian is hard to accept, but it is a clever dramatic device, and is made fairly plausible by Olivia's excited state, and the resemblance of the twins in speech, dress, features and behavior. Viola has played a perfect courtier in her disguise, Sebastian is one in reality. Hence, Olivia finds no difference between the twins, and

63

we may be sure that her recognition of her fortunate mistake will cause her no great anguish.

A modern audience must sometimes strain its credulity to accept the plausibility of the mistaken identity. In Shakespeare's day the problem was much simpler since male actors played both male and female roles.

ACT V · SCENE 1

Summary

The last act, consisting of one long scene, is a lengthy summing up of the complicated happenings of the four preceding acts. Most of the major characters except Maria appear in it at some time or other, in a series of rapidly changing situations.

Fabian and the Clown enter; Fabian asks to be shown the letter from Malvolio which Feste is taking to Olivia, but Feste is unwilling to let him see it. At that moment Orsino comes along, attended by Viola and Curio amongst others, and recognizing Feste, asks him how he is. Feste enters into jesting with him, and is given money by the Duke for his wit. He asks for more and succeeds in obtaining it, but is refused a third piece of gold and leaves to call Olivia. Meanwhile, Antonio is brought along by the police. Viola tells Orsino that he rescued her from the duel. Orsino recalls the last time he saw Antonio wreaking havoc among Orsino's fleet. One of the officers informs Orsino that, "This is that Antonio" who took a ship sailing from Crete, and occupied another in a battle in which Orsino's nephew, Titus, lost his leg. He states that Antonio was found fighting in the street. The Duke asks what brought Antonio to his town, into the midst of enemies. Antonio denies being a pirate, but affirms himself Orsino's enemy. He explains that Viola is the cause of his presence, that he saved her life, took care of her, followed her to the town and defended her against danger. He accuses Viola of "false cunning," that she refused him his purse and denied knowing him. Orsino asks, in amazement, when Viola came to the town, and Antonio's answer that for three months they lived by the seashore convinces him that he is lying, as Viola has served at his court for three months.

Olivia enters now and asks Orsino what he wants, except her love which she cannot give him. She turns to Viola, accusing her of breach of promise (Sebastian had promised to return shortly, Viola naturally knows of no such promise). Orsino cuts the answer short and pleads with Olivia in person. She still resists his suit, and he grows furious. His jealous love-sickness would prompt him to kill Olivia, but he decides upon a better revenge for Olivia's hard-heartedness. He has found out that Viola is wooed by Olivia and would "sacrifice the lamb that I do love" in order to spite Olivia's "raven's heart." Olivia feels herself imposed upon, for she has just been married to a man whom she took for Viola. She reminds Viola of it, calls for the priest, and calls Viola

"Cesario husband." She attempts to dispel Viola's fear of Orsino which makes her deny the marriage. The priest enters and confirms Olivia's words, stating that he performed the wedding ceremony only two hours before. Orsino is enraged, and leaves Viola to Olivia, telling Viola never to see him again. The crisis of the scene has been reached.

Sir Andrew enters, by good fortune and asks for a surgeon for himself and Sir Toby. He wails over the blows he has received from Sebastian. Accusingly, he points the finger at Viola as the culprit. Viola naturally denies having hurt him, as she thinks he is referring to the duel. Sir Toby staggers in with the Clown. Sir Toby is hurt too, but little affected by it. He comically abuses the surgeon when Feste says that he found him drunk. He leaves with the Clown, Fabian and Sir Andrew, calling the latter a fool and knave.

Unexpectedly, Sebastian returns from a search of the town for Antonio. He comes upon the crowd, ignorant of the confusion that his brief arrival and departure from the house has caused. He asks Olivia for pardon for his absence, noticing the strange look she gives him. The Duke and Olivia look in amazement at this second Cesario, like Viola in features, speech, dress and manner. Sebastian rushes to Antonio and greets him with joyous cries, "How have the hours rack'd and tortured me, Since I have lost thee!" Antonio asks him how he has divided himself into two identical persons; the Duke and Olivia comment in amazement on the resemblance of him to Viola. Sebastian, now aware of Viola, declares that he never had a brother and that his sister was drowned. She replies to his questions that she is of Messaline, and that her twin brother, Sebastian, was drowned; she is afraid that the man before her is a spirit come to frighten her. After further proof that each has found the twin believed lost, Viola promises to take him to the captain who has her clothes. Sebastian, turning to Olivia, explains to her that due to Nature's "bias" or predisposition, she has been wedded to him, not to Viola-Cesario. The Duke, recalling Viola's words that she would never love a woman as much as him, asks her hand in marriage and asks to see her as a woman. Viola's statement that the captain has been arrested by Malvolio reminds Olivia of her steward's distraction.

Fabian and the Clown return, and Feste starts reading Malvolio's letter in the tone of a madman, till Olivia angrily takes the letter from him and has it read by Fabian. She is accused in it of grievously wronging Malvolio, who insists on his sanity and states that he has the letter which made him act as he did. "This savours not much of distraction," comments Orsino. Fabian is sent after Malvolio, and while waiting for his return, the wedding-dates are fixed for the same day by Orsino and Olivia, who asks to have the celebration at her house.

Malvolio is brought along by Fabian. He repeats his charges in the letter, accusing his mistress of deliberately wronging him. She cannot deny the letter to be hers. He wishes to know the reason for giving him "such clear lights of favour," and then confining him in the cell and making him "the most notorious geck and gull." Olivia sees the similarity of the writing to hers; she is sure that Maria wrote it. She promises Malvolio justice and punishment of his enemies. Fabian reveals the reasons for Malvolio's gulling and those responsible for it. He takes the major blame on himself and Sir Toby, stating that Maria had little to do with it, except the writing of the letter, "in recompense whereof," Sir Toby has married her. Feste gives vent to his dislike of Malvolio by quoting from the letter by Maria, speaking of his own role as Sir Topas, and recalling Malvolio's taunt of his "barren wit." Malvolio leaves, swearing revenge on them all. Orsino asks that Malvolio be followed and questioned as to the whereabouts of the captain holding Viola's clothes. He invites himself into Olivia's house, with Viola, "Orsino's mistress and his fancy's queen."

They go off, in anticipation of a happy double ceremony, leaving Feste, who sings five stanzas of a song that begins:

> When that I was and a little tiny boy,
> With hey, ho, the wind and the rain,
> A foolish thing was but a toy,
> For the rain it raineth every day.

and ends:

> A great while ago the world begun,
> With hey, ho, the wind and the rain,
> But that's all one, our play is done,
> And we'll strive to please you every day.

Purpose

The entangled threads of the story are now smoothly tied in a double lover's knot. (It seems wise not to call this triple; Maria will, in all probability, as Toby once invited her, set her foot on her new husband's neck, to sober him.) And the audience is sent back from the world of masquerade and make-believe to the real world, where "the rain it raineth every day."

Notes

THE GENERAL AWAKENING

The recognition of Sebastian and his twin, Viola, brings about a general awakening, a sloughing off of the various pretenses and affectations of the play. Orsino and Olivia look upon one another, freed from their romantic mournfulness, as gentle friends. Even Sir Toby, though surly because of his wounds, abandons his mask of liking for Sir Andrew, and frankly calls him "an asshead and a coxcomb and a knave, a thin-faced knave, a gull!" Sir Andrew will go home a poorer but wiser man. Malvolio remains angry but is at least enlightened, and the Duke's words will be obeyed and "persuade him to a peace." It is only the

Fool's song — if we heed it, and the patter of its refrain — that reminds us we have been lingering in a world of dream.

VIOLA'S SILENCE

There are two points in this scene at which Viola could have explained the others' misunderstanding. At each of these — when Olivia first greets her, and when the Duke bids Cesario to go with Olivia and never see him again — Shakespeare provides a swift change of subject, to cover Viola's silence. The reason for silence, however, lies deeper than these shifts; they merely cover but do not explain it. To speak of Sebastian would mean that she must reveal her true sex, a disclosure that still seemed premature. Besides, Viola had earlier remarked that time must untangle the matter, "It is too hard a knot for me to untie." Since what Olivia says indicates that Sebastian is near at hand, the natural thing for Viola to do is to wait for him to appear, when their confrontation will make the whole matter clear. Her innate femininity, as well, impels her not to push matters, and she preserves what Bertrand Evans calls a "long, superb silence."

THE ENDING OF THE PLAY

While there is usually little doubt, in a comedy, as to what the end will be, we are often held interested by our wonder over how the end will be brought about. Clearly, here, it is the meeting of Sebastian and Viola that clears up the situation, and there the play might end. Shakespeare, however, is not inclined to end his plays at an emotional peak; he prefers to lessen the tension before he lets the audience go. He therefore has Viola say she will bring the captain who has her maiden garments, instead of "this my masculine usurp'd attire." She tells Sebastian:

> Do not embrace me till each circumstance
> Of place, time, fortune, do cohere and jump
> That I am Viola.

It is after this that Shakespeare puts, not only Orsino's declaration of love for Viola, but the entire story of the release of Malvolio, before Viola, and the others leave the stage free for Feste's final song.

PRIEST

In this play, every character has his moment. Even the priest, briefly introduced to witness the betrothal of Sebastian and Olivia, rises to his occasion, when he testifies before the Duke in his most dignified tones:

> A contract of eternal bond of love,
> Confirmed by mutual joinder of your hands,
> Attested by the holy close of lips,
> Strengthened by interchangement of your rings.
> And all the ceremony of this compact
> Sealed in my function, by my testimony.

Ironically undercutting this impressive utterance is the fact that the priest is also mistaking Cesario for Sebastian, and is thus unwittingly bearing false witness.

VARIETY OF DIALOGUE

Almost immediately, Shakespeare follows this pompous diction with the bloody, brawly, tipsy, lurching tale of Sir Andrew and Sir Toby.

The variety of dialogue Shakespeare offers us is indeed remarkable. Just before Olivia calls upon the priest for his testimony, there is a crackling exchange (six lines broken into eight utterances, emphasized by rhyme) as the Duke and Olivia both claim Cesario. Olivia protests that she has been beguiled:

> *Viola.* Who does beguile you? Who does do you wrong?
> *Olivia.* Hast thou forgot thyself? Is it so long?
> Call forth the holy Father.
> *Duke.*   Come, away!
> *Olivia.* Whither, my lord? Cesario, husband, stay.
> *Duke.* Husband!
> *Olivia.*   Ay, husband. Can he that deny?
> *Duke.* Her husband, sirrah!
> *Viola.*   No, my lord, not I.

It has been suggested that these words of Viola — "No, my lord, not I." — are less a protest than a whoop of victory. For with the word "husband" Viola must have grasped it all: Olivia and Sebastian are mated, and Orsino is freed to her. Time is indeed doing an excellent job!

ALLUSIONS

The exchange between Fabian and Feste at the beginning of the scene, regarding Malvolio's letter, contains a contemporary allusion:

> *Fabian.* Now, as thou lovest me, let me see his letter.
> *Feste.* Good master Fabian, grant me another request.
> *Fabian.* Anything.
> *Feste.* Do not desire to see this letter.
> *Fabian.* This is to give a dog, and in recompense desire my dog again.

The episode was recorded in Manningham's Diary two days after Queen Elizabeth died:

> Dr. Bullein, the Queen's kinsman, had a dog which he doted on, so much so that the Queen, understanding of it, requested he would grant her one desire, and he should have whatsoever he would ask. She demanded his dog; he gave it, and 'Now,

Madame,' quoth he, 'you promised to give me my desire.'
'I will,' quoth she. 'Then I pray you give me my dog again.'

This anecdote must have been widely current for Shakespeare to have tucked the allusion into the play. His using it, however, is another argument against the notion that the play was written expressly for the Queen, for it would have been impolite to thrust upon Her proud and hothead Majesty so blunt a reminder of an occasion when she was worsted. She would have done more than make the Victorian comment, "We are not amused."

When the Duke, hurt at Olivia's preferring his page to his lordship, contemplates revenge, he asks himself:

> Why should I not, had I the heart to do it,
> Like to the Egyptian thief at point of death,
> Kill what I love?

Little read today, but lively and quite readable, though longwinded, are the Greek romances of the second and third century. Among these is the *Ethiopica* of Heliodorus, which tells the story of Theagenes and Chariclea. This loving couple was captured by a band of robbers, headed by the Egyptian thief Thyamis, who fell madly in love with Chariclea. Attacked by a stronger band, Thyamis rushed into his cave to kill Chariclea, to make sure that she would be beside him in the next world. (However, in the dark, he plunged his sword into the breast of the wrong woman.) A translation of Heliodorus was licensed in 1568; an edition printed in 1587 was quite popular.

FESTE'S FINAL SONG

The song of Feste that concludes the play has been subjected to considerable critical comment. Early scholars have called it "wretched stuff," have said that it has no connection at all with the play, have even declared that it is none of Shakespeare's, but was tagged on by the actor who played the Fool, to amuse the groundlings. At the other extreme, it has been hailed as "the most philosophical Clown's song upon record," a capsule compendium of a man's life, from "tiny boy," through "man's estate," to palsied age ("unto my bed"), concluding that the time-bound generations move on alike — "A great while ago the world begun" — and that all are treated alike by impartial fate. The mild melancholy of the thought, tempered by the music and the glow of the departing lovers, makes the song a fit farewell to the gaiety of *Twelfth Night*, or *What You Will*.

Methods of Analyzing Characters

Describing the Characters

It is always a good idea to begin any commentary on characters with a brief description of each of them — what they are like, what they seem to think about themselves, etc. This kind of brief survey of the characters assures the student that he will not assume too much when discussing the characters in more complex or sophisticated ways. It also forces the student not to overlook any of the various characters' essential attributes. It should be pointed out that Hamlet is the young prince of Denmark, or that Othello is a Moor; then these simple facts should be amplified by whatever else we know. Also, if Shakespeare does not tell us a great deal about a particular character, this should be pointed out. If we do not learn enough about Sebastian it is perhaps because Shakespeare does not want to detract too much attention from Viola. All in all, then, one should make a short survey of the characteristics — both emotional and physical — of the characters.

Analysis of Character Development

Probably the most important aspect of character analysis is the treatment of the development of the characters, and primarily the main characters. It is all-important to explain how a character *changes* in the course of the play. And one must also explain *why* those changes take place *when* they do. Even if a character seems static throughout, there must be an explanation. It may be that Shakespeare is using the character as a prop, a necessary convenience, or simply as an illustrative example of an alternative to the mode of existence courted by the hero or heroine. When certain emotions — such as greed, hate, love, revenge, bitterness, confidence — come to the surface, we should try to understand precisely how and why. Is there violent reaction or calm acceptance? Does Lady Macbeth's incipient guilt plunge her into a quasi-psychotic depression? The basic changes, not the minor ones, should be briefly delineated and more thoroughly analyzed. Is it right that a certain character feels as he does? Is it human or is it extreme? Abnormal or normal? Unusual or typical? Surprising or expected? Are changes foreshadowed? Are they ever illogical or too contrived? All literary analysis consists of an extended process of asking questions and this questioning process is particularly vital to the analysis of characters. We must understand why characters behave and change in order to understand the meaning of the entire play. Aside from all the usual reasons that characters change, as, for example, when one's mother or relative is killed and one suddenly is filled with a desire for revenge and acts accordingly, many explanations of character change can be found either in their motivation, as it is developed by the dramatist, or by the demands of the themes. And these will be our next two considerations.

Motivation

In considering the motivation of characters we are fundamentally enlarging our answer to the "why" of character behavior. Shakespeare is of course very "modern" in his grasp of human psychology and the ways in which thought should be translated into action. For example, we recall that the original exciting action of *Twelfth Night* is Viola's desire to disguise herself as a boy. But this does not explain everything. Remember that she also expressed a keen interest in Orsino, even before she met him. Perhaps she knew from the outset that she would try to win his love. In other words, in discussing motivation, we are trying to describe, as extensively as possible, the total psychological make-up of a character. Then we discover and interpret his or her uniqueness through the actions brought about by psychology. Sometimes there is an absence of motivation; at least there *appears* to be such an absence (and let us not, like Othello, think that things are what they seem). In any case, no survey of a play's characters would be complete without explanations of behavior.

Thematic Characters

Often we discover that the behavior of certain characters can be explained by themes. That is, a character like Malvolio may act in selfish ways consistently because allegorically he represents selfishness. Any character in any play may be thought of as a thematic character from one point of view or another, but we generally limit our use of the term to characters who clearly represent certain dominant abstractions which are clashing in a play — i.e., good and evil, love and hatred, loyalty and disloyalty, faithfulness and unfaithfulness (notice how all are extensions of good and evil). Few comedies involve thematic characters, but it is a notion that we should be aware of. In general, it is better to search for what is human or unique about certain characters, but it is always worthwhile to mention briefly the thematic possibilities of the characters. Why are they in the play? Why do they behave as they do? How does their behavior demonstrate particular ideas?

Analyzing Character Relationships

Although inherent in the other methods, the analysis of the relationships between the characters can be used as complete analysis in itself. The world of the play is largely defined by the nature of the different relationships. Viola has very specific and unusual relationships with both Orsino and Olivia, for example, and the two relationships show us different things about Viola, on the one hand, and confirm some of the same things on the other. Feste is both a clown and a conspirator; Maria is more than just Olivia's servant. The "more" or the "less" of the basic relationships of friendship, marriage, command, etc., must be clarified, for through this clarification of relationships, we arrive at a greater understanding of the characters themselves.

Character Sketches

Viola

Viola is the real heroine of the play. It is of her adventures, her love and her modesty, her beauty and her patience that we think when the play is mentioned. The other serious characters, Olivia, Orsino, Sebastian, derive what interest they possess chiefly from their connection with Viola.

HER BEAUTY

It is not Shakespeare's method to "give out divers schedules" of the beauty of his heroines. He does not paint them in parcels, "as, item, two lips, indifferent red; item, two grey eyes, with lids to them; item, one neck, one chin, and so forth." He lets his characters speak for themselves and for each other, and his readers form their own conclusions. References to Viola's personal appearance are numerous. These allusions, helped out by the reader's own imagination, will enable each to form his own conception of the personal charms of the heroine. It matters little that no two persons' conceptions will be alike. No two persons looking at a beautiful scene see alike; but to each the scene is beautiful, though in different degrees according to the beholder. The Duke thus speaks of Viola in her boy's disguise:

> Diana's lip
> Is not more smooth and rubious; thy small pipe
> Is as the maiden's organ, shrill and sound,
> And all is semblative a woman's part. (Act I, Sc. 4, 32-35)

Maria calls Cesario a "fair young man" (Act I, Sc. 5, 111). Even Malvolio, whom no one would accuse of partiality towards any one except himself, describes the youth as being "very well-favoured" (Act I, Sc. 5, 174). Olivia no sooner sees him than she feels his "perfections with an invisible and subtle stealth to creep in at her eyes" (Act I, Sc. 5, 322-324).

She is impressed with his air of distinction:

> "What is your parentage?"
> "Above my fortunes, yet my state is well:
> I am a gentleman." "I'll be sworn thou art;
> Thy tongue, thy face, thy limbs, actions and spirit,
> Do give thee five-fold blazon." (Act I, Sc. 5, 314-18)

Not even anger (tempered, no doubt, by pity for the Countess) mars the beauty of expression of the youth:

> O, what a deal of scorn looks beautiful
> In the contempt and anger of his lip! (Act III, Sc. 1, 161-2)

Sebastian, modestly, describes his sister as:

> A lady, sir, though it was said she much resembled me, was
> yet of many accounted beautiful; but, though I could not
> with such estimable wonder overfar believe that, yet thus far
> I will boldly publish her; she bore a mind that envy could not
> but call fair.
>
> (Act II, Sc. 1, 26-30)

Sir Toby, who in his sober moments was worldly-wise, if nothing
else, tells us that, "the behaviour of the young gentleman gives him out
to be of good capacity and breeding" (Act III, Sc. 4, 202-3).

HER WOMANLINESS AND SYMPATHY

Self-forgetfulness is one of her most beautiful and most pervading
characteristics. Her sympathy extends to all her sex and to all lovers. She
knows, she says, "Too well what love women to men may owe" (Act II,
Sc. 4, 106). With a woman's quick instinct she perceives that she is loved
by Olivia, and her heart goes out to her rival in womanly pity:

> As I am woman,—now alas the day!—
> What thriftless sighs shall poor Olivia breathe. (Act I, Sc. 2, 39-40)

She can even forget her own great love for the Duke in pity for his
hopeless passion for Olivia. Indeed, his forlorn condition was probably
one of his chief attractions to her gentle heart. She possessed a natural
curiosity to see the face of the woman who could inspire the Duke with
such a longing, and she has tact enough to discover the means whereby
to gratify her curiosity. The proud lady who has sworn that "like a
cloistress, she will veiled-walk" for seven long years is unable to
maintain her reserve before the mingled flattery, wit and determination
of the youthful messenger of love.

HER MODESTY

Her modesty permeates all her speech and is revealed in all her
actions. She assumes the disguise of a page as protection, but she takes
no pleasure in playing a part:

> Disguise, I see, thou art a wickedness,
> Wherin the pregnant enemy does much.   (Act II, Sc. 2, 28-9)

She is no Amazon, being "one that had rather go with sir priest
than sir knight," but in circumstances which to her mind were filled with
the gravest danger to herself, her modesty prevented her from speaking
and openly declaring her sex. Although filled with the deepest love for
Orsino, she "never told her love," but with exquisite delicacy conveyed
to the Duke a suggestion of it in such a manner that only in the excep-
tional and improbable circumstances which actually occurred could he
become aware of it.

HER LOVE

For purity, tenderness and self-sacrificing devotion she might serve as a model to all lovers. She knows from her own experience that the Duke is speaking the truth when he says of his own sex:

> Our fancies are more giddy and unfirm,
> More longing, wavering, sooner lost and worn,
> Than women's are.   (Act II, Sc. 4, 33-35)

The state of her own heart is truly described in the memorable lines in which she replies to the Duke's question,

"And what's her history?"

> "A blank, my lord. She never told her love,
> But let concealment, like a worm i' the bud,
> Feed on her damask cheek: she pined in thought,
> And with a green and yellow melancholy
> She sat like Patience on a monument,
> Smiling at grief."   (Act II, Sc. 4, 111-115)

Such was the constancy of Viola towards the object of her devotion, and even so, she would have endured to the end had not fate been kinder to her than she dared to hope for herself.

She knows that love cannot be forced where no germ of affection already exists:

> Say that some lady, as perhaps there is,
> Hath for your love a greater pang of heart
> As you have for Olivia: you cannot love her;
> You tell her so; must she not then be answer'd?
>   (Act II, Sc. 4, 90-93)

and yet she knows (as the Duke did not), how an aspiring lover should behave:

> If I did love you in my master's flame,
> With such a suffering, such a deadly life,
> In your denial I would find no sense;
> I would not understand it.   (Act I, Sc. 5, 290-293)

Being a woman she could only suffer and be patient; had she been a man she would have known how to move heaven and earth to win her end.

Her love for her brother is, in its kind, as strong and tender as that which she felt for Orsino. Her first uttered thought after the shipwreck was for Sebastian. Before she knew Olivia she was attracted to her because of her reported devotion to the brother she had lost. But there is a difference between the two ladies. Olivia makes a rash vow in order "to season a brother's dead love, which she would keep fresh and lasting in her sad remembrance" (Act I, Sc. 1, 30-32), and only once speaks of him throughout the play; Viola makes no vow, but plainly shows that her brother, whom she thought dead, was ever present to her memory,

Prove true, imagination, O, prove true,
That I, dear brother, be now ta'en for you!

(Act III, Sc. 4, 414-415)

RESOURCEFULNESS AND DETERMINATION

Viola is cast into a difficult part. She is in a strange land, without her brother whom she must believe lost, even though the captain tells her that he may still be alive. Most of her possessions are gone. Her situation is worse, since she is a woman (it was not considered becoming for a woman then to go unattended). Viola is forced to make her own way in Illyria. She displays resourcefulness and firmness in her quick acceptance of each new situation. She hears of Olivia and would like to serve her until such time that she can make known her "estate" or rank. She changes her mind when the captain presents to her the difficulties of gaining access to Olivia. Instead, she enters Orsino's service. Her intelligence and skill in music and singing win her master's quick favor. She carries out her errand to Olivia successfully. She is a match for Malvolio; he complains that she is "fortified against any denial" (Act I, Sc. 5, 137). She persuades Olivia to grant her a private hearing and to unveil her face. She plays her two-fold part as man and as love-messenger so well that no one suspects her identity. She threatens Sir Toby that she will ask him for an escort from Olivia, and prepares to fight the duel only out of fear that otherwise her identity may be revealed. She resists Olivia's wooing as best she can, without giving herself away. She maintains her poise in the face of Antonio's charges of ingratitude. Throughout, she plays her difficult part to the best of her ability, knowing that once Orsino discovers her disguise, he may turn her out. Only at the critical point in the last act does she think that all is lost and she begins to give up hope.

INTELLIGENCE AND WIT

Her daring in dressing as a page and taking service with the Duke is accompanied by lively intelligence. She makes good use of her musical accomplishments, her good breeding, and her skill in conversation, in order to make herself the Duke's close confidante and companion. She humors him successfully in his sentimental moods. She is practical and businesslike in her conversation with the captain, seeking information about Illyria. She readily falls in with Feste's jests when she calls at the house in Act III. In her interviews with Olivia, she is practical, impersonal, witty, sympathetic and personal in turn. She plays the courtier, using pompous phrases like "most radiant taxation of homage," "most excellent, accomplis'd lady, the heavens exquisite, and unmatchable beauty," "bring no overture of war, no rain odours on you." She maintains dignity in resisting Olivia's advances, Maria's impertinence is demolished by her sarcastic reply (Act I, Sc. 5, 192). She is dignified towards Sir Toby who bears the challenge for the duel.

HER MORAL CHARACTER

She loves the Duke as only she can love, and yet, when he employs her to urge his suit with another lady, she does not for a moment hesitate to do that which, however unacceptable, was in her eyes a clear duty:

> I'll do my best
> To woo your lady: [Aside] yet a barful strife?
> Whoe'er I woo myself would be his wife.   (Act I, Sc. 4, 41-43)

Nor does she perform her duty in a half-hearted manner, but does all that she could in such a service on another's behalf. In the last scene, her sense of duty and her modesty forbid her to speak in her own defence when her master is present, desiring to press his suit in person. Olivia twice addresses her, and asks her to speak, but her only answer is "My lord would speak, my duty hushes me."

Not even to save her life will she reveal herself until she "had made her own occasion mellow," but to give ease to Orsino she will "most jocund, apt and willingly" die a thousand deaths.

Olivia

She is not introduced directly, but by repeated references in the first scenes: the captain remarks of her and Orsino; Maria and Sir Toby furnish us with further background information. She is more complex than Viola, following a less single-minded course of action, and more changeable in temper and emotion.

We do not at once and unhesitatingly form an opinion of her. Our first impressions become modified on a second and third reading of the play, and different readers will express different judgments with regard to her actions and her character. At first we think of her as being proud, then we find her casting herself and her fortune at the feet of a page. We think of her as being loyal in affectionate memory for a lost brother, yet she makes a rash vow and breaks it within a very few days. She refuses to receive one messenger from the Duke, and yet admits the next, who is rather more insistent. She pretends to be immune to flattery, and we feel that Viola's tactful flattery at their first interview was not without its effect upon her. Some of these changes and apparent inconsistencies must, no doubt, be attributed to the transforming power of love, but others we must attribute to her fickle nature.

PERSONAGE AND APPEARANCE

She is a wealthy, high-ranking countess, beautiful, and in every respect she is apparently the most ideal match for the Duke. She has been orphaned by her father's death a year before the play takes place; her brother's more recent death has left her without relatives except for her uncle, Sir Toby, who also is a kind of nominal guardian. In reality, she administers her estate herself.

She is considered to be beautiful by all. Orsino speaks of her appearance as purging "the air of pestilence," Viola calls her beauty "truly blent, whose red and white Nature's own sweet and cunning hand laid on," and addresses Olivia as "Fair cruelty" and "If you were the devil, you are fair." Orsino calls out at her approach in Act V, "Now heaven walks on earth."

SHE INSPIRES RESPECT

Up to the period of the opening of the play she has evidently lived a life of noble self-restraint and gained an honorable name with persons of all classes. The captain speaks of her as "a virtuous maid." Sebastian is struck with the manner in which she can "sway her house, command her followers":

> Take and give back affairs and their despatch
> With such a smooth, discreet and stable bearing
> As I perceives she does. (Act IV, Sc. 3, 18-20)

Even when she loses her heart to the page and no longer "owns herself," she preserves her dignity. Earnest in her appeals, beseeching as she is, she never altogether loses her respect for herself, and as a consequence she never forfeits ours. She humbles her pride, and will do anything to win Viola's love, provided she may keep her honor safe:

> What shall you ask of me that I'll deny,
> That honour saved, may upon asking give. (Act III, Sc. 4, 231-2)

HER SERVANTS ARE DEVOTED TO HER

We are given an insight into the manner in which she inspires a sentiment of loyalty in those by whom she is habitually surrounded. She can criticize them when necessary, and even speak severely to them upon occasion, but she has their interests always at heart. She speaks plainly to the Clown in his presence and scolds him for his errors, but she will not allow others to speak ill of him:

> Thou has spoke for us, madonna, as if thy eldest son
> Should be a fool. (Act I, Sc. 5, 122-3)

She tells Malvolio his faults to his face when he assumes too much (Act I, Sc. 5, 98), but when he appears to have taken leave of his senses, she is all gentleness and consideration for him, "God comfort thee!" she says, and "Heaven restore thee." And again:

> Let some of my people have a special care of him; I would
> Not have him miscarry for the half of my dowry.
> (Act III, Sc. 4, 67-9)

In the case of Sir Toby, she shows her displeasure, but cannot forget that he is her kinsman. When angered by an insult to her lover she can be severe enough, "Hold, Toby; on thy life I charge thee, hold!"

(Act IV, Sc. 1, 49). And when he makes as though he would protest, she speaks more strongly:

> Will it be ever thus? Ungracious wretch,
> Fit for the mountains and the barbarous caves,
> Where manners ne'er were preach'd! out of my sight!
>
> (Act IV, Sc. 1, 51-3)

Strict justice and occasional severity, softened by a genuine interest in and affection for her dependants, appear to be her ruling principles in the conduct of her household. At the end she is ready to acknowledge that Malvolio has been "notoriously abused," and offers to make him "both the plaintiff and the judge" of his own cause.

HER LOVE

Her love comes to her as a kind of punishment for her coldness. She herself calls it "a most extracting frenzy," and, indeed, it seems more like a madness than anything else. She is fully conscious of the unreasonableness of it and attempts to fight against it, but finds it irresistible. She is the last person one would have expected to "fall in love at first sight." But for once she is mastered by a greater passion than her pride. She would have concealed her love (as Viola did hers), but her control over herself is not equal to the task:

> A murderous guilt shows not itself more soon
> Than love that would seem hid: love's night is noon.
>
> (Act III, Sc. 1, 163-4)

That she does strive against this mastering passion is evident from her words:

> I have said too much unto a heart of stone,
> And laid mine honour too unchary on't:
> There's something in me that reproves my fault;
> But such a headstrong potent fault it is,
> That it but mocks reproof.   (Act III, Sc. 4, 221-5)

The futility of struggling she expresses in language strong enough in itself, but acquiring additional force on the lips of one who was always sober and careful in her conversation: "A friend like thee might bear my soul to hell" (Act III, Sc. 4, 237).

Maria

Maria is the source of much of the comic action in the play. She enjoys seeing people humiliated and made uncomfortable. Her function, like that of most comedy, is to expose the faults, vanities and ignorance of her fellow creatures in a pleasant way. She unmasks Malvolio's vanity, reveals the depths of the ignorance and folly of Sir Andrew, and

78

acts as an encouragement to the boisterous humor of Sir Toby and the wit of Feste.

PERSONAGE AND APPEARANCE

She is called Olivia's handmaid, that is to say, her closest attendant and something of a companion and confidante. Her intimacy with her mistress and the trust placed in her are shown in her repeated scolding of other members of the household: of Feste when he returns from his carousing about town; of Sir Toby for his drinking and Sir Andrew's companionship; and of the three companions for their carousing late at night. She appears to be of noble birth and well educated, as her relative intimacy with Olivia, her familiarity with Sir Toby and Sir Andrew, and her skill in writing the letter to Malvolio, show.

We are told little of her appearance except that she is small. Viola's uncertainty (Act I, Sc. 5) as to which is the lady of the house implies that in looks and conduct Maria is of good social origin. Her small height is insisted on repeatedly. Viola calls her "giant"; Sir Toby refers to her as "Penthesilea," the Queen of the Amazons, as the "Youngest wren of nine," and calls her "little Villain." The reference to the Queen of the Amazons implies, moreover, that Maria is formidable in spite of her small size.

HER WIT

No one is safe from her mischievous wit. She so confuses the feeble mind of Sir Andrew, and makes him appear so ridiculous, that Sir Toby exclaims:

> O knight, thou lackest a cup of canary: when did I see
> thee so put down? (Act I, Sc. 3, 87)

She tries to tease Feste, but in him she meets her match, for though she wins commendation from him for her wit, she obtains little other satisfaction out of him. Neither does she succeed with Viola, but in this case she was perhaps deterred by the presence of her mistress, Olivia (Act I, Sc. 5, 101-3). Above all things she delights in teasing Malvolio. She has made him her study, and knows him through and through; she knows how to turn his failings to account so well that when she teases him he falls with the utmost readiness into the net she has prepared for him:

> For Monsieur Malvolio, let me alone with him: if I do not
> gull him into a nayword, and make him a common recreation,
> do not think I have wit enough to lie straight in my bed: I
> know I can do it. (Act I, Sc. 3, 152-6)

She is as good as her word, and carries out every item of her plan. Then, with what gusto does she watch the success of her practical joke! She dogs him "like his murderer." With what infectious merriment she communicates to her partners in the plot the successful progress of its development! She taunts Malvolio, and torments him, and goads him to frenzy without ever the smallest feeling of remorse. The angrier he becomes the more she rejoices. She does not give him a moment's rest, "Nay, pursue him now, lest the device take air and taint." (Act III, Sc. 4, 140-1).

HER CLEVERNESS

She is good at reading character and especially at finding weak spots. She gauges accurately the depth of Sir Andrew's folly (Act I, Sc. 3). She knows how to win and to keep the admiration of Sir Toby, who is vehement in his praises of her lively wit and brilliant inventive powers:

> She's a beagle, true-bred, and one that adores me: what o' that? (Act II, Sc. 3, 203)

And again:

> I could marry this wench for this device . . . and ask no other dowry with her but such another jest. (Act II, Sc. 5, 200)

Finally, he declares that he will follow her "To the gates of Tartar, thou most excellent devil of wit!" (Act II, Sc. 5, 227).

Given such a disposition on the part of the knight, we are not surprised when with cunning flattery she ends up marrying him.

Even Feste, a master in the "corrupting of words," applauds Maria's witty remarks and praises her skilful diplomacy:

> Apt, in good faith; very apt. Well, go thy way; if Sir Toby would leave drinking, thou wert as witty a piece of Eve's flesh as any in Illyria. (Act I, Sc. 5, 29-32)

She not only invents the plot against Malvolio, she chooses also the most opportune moment for setting it in motion. She acts as stage manager in her comedy, and gives out the parts to be played by each of her fellow-conspirators. She shows a genius for detail and contrives so that Malvolio "does obey every point of the letter that I dropped to betray him."

In Olivia's presence she behaves in such a manner that although she has been the plotter of the deception, she herself is never once suspected, and she plays her hand so well that when the plot is brought to light, her fellow-conspirators take upon themselves the blame and beg (and no doubt obtain) forgiveness for her, on the ground that she was justified in all she did by some "stubborn and uncourteous parts" in the character of Malvolio:

> Maria writ
> The letter at Sir Toby's great importance;
> In recompense whereof he hath married her.
> How with a sportful malice it was follow'd,
> May rather pluck on laughter than revenge;

If that the injuries be justly weigh'd
That have on both sides pass'd.   (Act V, Sc. 1, 374-380)

Orsino

He is well spoken of by all persons, for he is elegant, refined,
virtuous and highly accomplished. The captain voices the general
opinion of him when he terms him "A noble duke, in nature as in
name" (Act I, Sc. 2, 25). Olivia is by no means blind to his charms
although she cannot love him. Yet, she says:

> I suppose him virtuous, know him noble
> Of great estate, of fresh and stainless youth;
> In voices well divulged, free, learn'd and valiant
> And in dimension and the shape of nature
> A gracious person.   (Act I, Sc. 5, 284-8)

He possesses an exquisite taste for music, and is deeply versed in the
language of love. He is open-handed and generous, and sufficiently
varied in his tastes to derive pleasure from the society of Feste as well as
from that of Viola who can talk "masterly" of love. But all these
qualities are more or less superficial. If we want to know what his real
character was we must probe deeper.

HIS REAL CHARACTER

He is a sentimentalist. He affects fine feeling and exquisite
sensibility. He can talk of love, but cannot act as a lover in his circumstances should have acted. He is inconsistent in word and action. At one
moment he says:

> For, boy, however we do praise ourselves,
> Our fancies are more giddy and unfirm,
> More longing, wavering, sooner lost and worn,
> Than women's are.   (Act II, Sc. 4, 32-35)

and a few moments later he describes the love of women as mere
"appetite":

> No motion of the liver, but the palate,
> That suffer surfeit, cloyment and revolt;
> But mine is all as hungry as the sea,
> And can digest as much.   (Act II, Sc. 4, 99-102)

He calls for music from the Fool and after an instant is satiated
with it. He is "unstaid and skittish," dreamy and rapturous, and lacking
in balance. The Fool was a good judge of character and has this to say of
people who are so lacking in stability:

> Now, the melancholy god protect thee; and the tailor make
> thy doublet of changeable taffeta, for thy mind is a very opal. I
> would have men of such constancy put to sea, that their business

might be everything and their intent everywhere; for that's it that always makes a good voyage of nothing.   (Act II, Sc. 4, 73-79)

When the mystery of Viola's sex was cleared up he experienced no difficulty in transferring his affections at once from Olivia to his former page and making her his "mistress and his fancy's queen."

His language is typical of his sentimentality; it is highly-colored, rich and poetical. He speaks of violets, scented winds, rich golden shafts of love, of beds of flowers, of the pleasure in music. He compares his own capacity with the sea twice (Act I, Sc. 1, 10-11; Act II, Sc. 4, 99). He is always praising love, its sweetness, luxury, melancholy, constancy and fervor. He compares Olivia to a deity, "now heaven walks on earth" (Act V, Sc. 1, 95).

Sebastian

He is only a minor character, of importance in bringing about the resolution of the plot, but otherwise playing no special part in the play. In the few appearances which he makes, however, he is characterized with surprising detail. We learn that he is Viola's twin, not merely in date of birth, but also in looks, dress, speech and conduct. "One face, one voice, one habit, and two persons" (Act V, Sc. 1, 212) is Orsino's comment on the twins' likeness. We first hear of him from the captain of the shipwrecked vessel:

> I saw your brother,
> Most provident in peril, bind himself,
> Courage and hope both teaching him the practice,
> To a strong mast that lived upon the sea;
> Where, like Arion on the dolphin's back,
> I saw him hold acquaintance with the waves
> So long as I could see.   (Act I, Sc. 2, 11-17)

When first we met with him he was in the company of another captain, Antonio, who has been instrumental in saving him from drowning. He is overcome with sorrow at the supposed death of his sister, but does not forget to express his deep gratitude to his deliverer, whom he is unwilling to burden with the weight of his own misfortunes. His youthful and adventurous nature, however, does not permit him to brood in solitude over his sorrows. He goes forth to "satisfy his eyes with the memorials and the things of fame that do renown the city." Adventures come to him without his seeking them, and find him ready for whatever may happen. He is quick in resolve and acts with promptness in every emergency, whether the task is to rid himself of the Clown, to use his fists upon Sir Andrew or his sword against Sir Toby, or to respond to the unexpected advances of the beautiful Olivia. Sir Andrew pays an eloquent tribute to his skill and vigor in sword practice:

> We took him for a coward, but he's the very devil incar-
> dinate.   (Act I, Sc. 1, 185-6)

Yet we must not suppose that he would enter into a brawl merely for the sake of fighting. He makes his excuses to Olivia:

> I am sorry, madam, I have hurt your kinsman;
> But, had it been the brother of my blood,
> I must have done no less with wit and safety.

(Act V, Sc. 1, 218-220)

He is a youth of few words, but of "right noble blood," and we feel sure that Olivia in marrying him will never have cause to regret the curious complications and comic accidents which led to such a result.

Sir Toby Belch

One of Shakespeare's most wonderful characteristics was his ability to present his characters in such a manner that we take the most charitable view of them. Sir Toby is an example in point; he is sly, impudent, coarse, indulgent and bullying, and yet we can hardly help liking him. His redeeming features are his wit and humor and his readiness to fight when necessary, and these characteristics almost nullify his many vices.

HE IS A BOISTEROUS DRUNKARD

His opening words, "I am sure care's an enemy to life," prepare us to know him. He keeps "ill hours," wastes his time "quaffing and drinking" with a foolish knight whom he makes the butt of his wit at the same time that he fleeces him of his money. He is either drunk or half-drunk through all the action of the play, and measures other people's merits by their powers of drinking. "I'll drink to my niece," he says:

> As long as there is a passage in my throat and drink in
> Illyria: he's a coward and a coystrill that will not drink to
> my niece till his brains turn o' the toe like a parish top.

(Act I, Sc. 3, 41-44)

He turns his niece's house into a drinking house, and comes into her presence disgustingly intoxicated. He shows no respect for people, calls Olivia a "Cataian" and bids Malvolio to "go hang." He cheats Sir Andrew out of his fortune and his horse, grey Capilet, and is an unblushing liar. But he thinks himself shrewder than he really is. Feste tells us that he "has a most weak pia mater," and Maria manipulates him into marrying her.

Underbred and of bad manners, as he is in reality, he is nevertheless able to impose upon Sir Andrew, who looks upon him with respect. He can recognize the "good capacity and breeding" of Cesario, and rightly perceives how Sir Andrew's ignorant challenge would strike the youth.

VIEW OF LIFE AND MENTALITY

His view of life is appropriately stated in his disapproval of Olivia's undue grief: "Nay I am sure care's an enemy to life" (Act I, Sc. 3, 2). He is full of life, giving vent to it in great drinking bouts lasting deep into the night, in a series of pranks, and in noisy singing and jesting. He is very selfish in the pursuit of his pleasure; he has no consideration for the feelings of Olivia, Malvolio, Sir Andrew, or Viola. His enjoyment of life is not otherwise selfish; he is expansive, fond of merry companionship, and is happiest when engaging in a joke with others. He is fond of teasing people. His constant drinking is evidence of his total lack of seriousness and prevents him from any very clear thinking, except in his pranks. His ability in thinking up schemes and his love for joking shows, however, an intelligence rather limited in application but lively and active.

HUMOR

In contrast to the more subtle wit of Maria and Feste, Sir Toby's brain exerts itself in the broad humor of farce and nonsense. He is fond of using words of his own making or application, "Tobyisms" like "substractors," "Castiliano vulgo," "cubiculo firago." He makes crude puns on the meanings of "confine" and "except." He baffles Sir Andrew by terms like "accost" and "pourquoi." He teases Maria by his sarcastic praise of Sir Andrew's qualities and knowledge of languages, and he makes fun of Sir Andrew, by commending his hair and his dancing and by instructing him how to challenge Viola (Act III, Sc. 2, 30-45). His language is remarkable for its flow and energy of expression rather than for wit. His most brilliant saying is his contemptuous remark to Malvolio, "Dost thou think, because thou are virtuous, there shall be no more cakes and ale?" He is the first to suggest Malvolio's punishment, though he is not responsible for the letter. He torments Malvolio (Act III, Sc. 4) by treating him like one possessed by the devil, and bears responsibility for locking him in the cell. He loves comic songs. The duel between Sir Andrew and Viola is arranged by him out of sheer love of practical jokes. He likes Maria for the fun that she sets in motion with the letter; he would marry her and ask no other dowry from her but such another jest (Act II, Sc. 5, 68).

Sir Andrew Aguecheek

He provides an effective contrast to Sir Toby in looks and character. The two knights are so well grouped together that their pecularities appear more absurd. Sir Toby is loud, boisterous, full of life and humorous invention, and brave; Sir Andrew is shallow, stupid, imitative and cowardly.

He is a wealthy knight, come to woo Olivia, without any knowledge on her part, it seems. He dimly perceives that he is wasting his time, but Sir Toby persuades him to stay on at the house.

Of his personal appearance we gather by his name that he is thin and pale-faced, and Sir Toby's comparison of his hair with the flax on a distaff shows it to be fair, long and straight. His voice is probably weak and shrill; Maria speaks of his dry hand, implying his physical weakness, though he calls himself a great eater of beef.

STUPIDITY

Sir Andrew's feeble and passive mind is his most outstanding characteristic. He states himself "many do call me fool" (Act II, Sc. 5, 74), and attributes his defect to the eating of beef, for "that does harm to my wit" (Act I, Sc. 3, 81). A man of means, he has been trained in the knightly accomplishments of dancing and fencing, and has spent his time on them and on bear-baiting. His education is poor; he regrets that he has not studied the arts. The letter of challenge to Viola is typical of his illogical, badly-functioning mind. He does not know the meaning of "pourquoi," though Sir Toby ironically informs Maria of his knowledge of three or four languages. He uses Sir Toby as a model to copy in conduct and speech; he picks up terms from Viola, "pregnant, couchsafed, odours," in order to increase his poor education. His shallow mind makes him incapable of seeing Sir Toby's shady purpose in making him stay on at Olivia's house. He is easily taken in by the explanation which Sir Toby and Fabian make of Olivia's favors to Viola. He prides himself on scorning "policy" or intrigue, whereas he is in reality too stupid to attempt it (Act III, Sc. 2, 27-28). Sir Toby's frightening report of Viola's fierceness is swallowed by him without hesitation (Act III, Sc. 4, 260). His opinions of others are based on the most superficial observation. He calls Viola a "rare courtier" (Act II, Sc. 1, 87) because of the affected speech she uses. He admires Feste for his sheer nonsense, not for his wit (Act II, Sc. 3, 20-28). He looks up to Sir Toby.

LACK OF ORIGINALITY

Sir Andrew's negative personality is brought out in his constant aping and parroting of others. He follows Sir Toby in everything, is provoked into giving his hand to Maria, into dancing, drinking, singing, and dueling. He suggests the singing of a catch, and conceives the feeble idea of challenging Malvolio to a duel and then walking out of it. Otherwise, he is always taking his lead from others, especially Sir Toby who has him completely under his thumb.

Feste

The court jester is an ancient institution, still of uncommon occurrence in Shakespeare's time. The fools, dressed in their distinctive costumes, were obliged to keep their masters amused with their wit and clowning. The jester was given considerable licence to speak his frank opinion to those present, and to make satirical observations on society. Successful fooling called for considerable mental alertness, power of observation, and nimble skill in words. Viola speaks on the wisdom of fools:

This fellow's wise enough to play the fool;

And to do that well craves a kind of wit:
He must observe their mood on whom he jests,
The quality of persons, and the time,
And, like'the haggard, check at every feather
That comes before his eye. This is a practice
As full of labour as a wise man's art:
For folly that he wisely shows is fit;
But wise men, folly fall'n, quite taint their wit.

(Act III, Sc. 1, 51-59)

SKILL

Feste is not ashamed of his calling; he explains to Olivia, "I wear not motley in my brain" (Act I, Sc. 5, 46), and "better a witty fool than a foolish wit" (Act I, Sc. 5, 27). His liberty as professional jester enables him prove to Olivia that she is a fool, allows him to tell Orsino of this inconstancy and restlessness to his face, "thy mind is a very opal," and to answer Maria's complaints by hinting at her designs on Sir Toby. Except for Malvolio, most of the characters appreciate his jesting, even when it is directed against them. He shows his versatility by acting the part of Sir Topas, the curate, before Malvolio. He is one of Shakespeare's most musical fools; he tells the Duke that he takes pleasure in singing. He sings two beautiful songs and joins in Sir Toby's revelry, leading in the catches, and falls in with Sir Toby's musical dialogue before the steward. He always carries his tabor or small drum with him.

WIT AND HUMOR

The clown's chief requirement, verbal wit, usually consists of quibbling and punning. Malvolio claims that Feste's wit is barren, and that he is not spontaneous, but has to be provided with a lead for his wit. Feste's bitter resentment of the charge shows that it is partly true. He is, however, capable of quick improvisation, shown by his ready winning of Olivia's favor after her annoyance with him in Act I, Scene 5. He quotes Latin readily; invents imaginary names like Quinapalus and talks pure nonsense, as in his talk of Pigrogromitus and the Vapians (Act II, Sc. 3, 21-27). He is fond of using comical logical reasoning; he proves Olivia a fool, proves to Viola that he is not Olivia's fool, and wins Orsino's praise for showing that he is worse off for his friends (Act V, Sc. 1, 16-22).

DEFECTS OF CHARACTER

Feste is rather loose-living; he is fond of taking part in the midnight revels of Sir Toby, and keeps loose company, as Sir Andrew's sending him sixpence for his "leman" seems to suggest. His resentment of Malvolio shows him to be spiteful. His attempts to wheedle money out of everyone are evidence of greediness, though he is dependent for his living on those he entertains with his wit.

Malvolio

It is worthy of note that the characters of the subplot, Sir Toby, Sir Andrew, Maria, and Malvolio, seem to be most closely drawn from certain social types of Shakespeare's day. The chief characters of the main plot are more idealized and more truly natives of the romantic, indefinite setting of Illyria; Sir Toby is much like a hearty, jovial country-squire; Sir Andrew is a bragging, cowardly knight, a common comic character; Malvolio is a type of snobbish Puritan. King James I, who intensely disliked the Puritans, had the play renamed *Malvolio*. The steward is given more truly satirical treatment than any other character. In spite of his evident good qualities, he is objectionable in a way that no other character in the play is, and he receives little sympathy. He earns some sympathy for his cruel punishment, but forfeits it by his last words of revenge. His name hints at his character: the "malevolent" or "bearing ill-will."

PERSONAGE AND APPEARANCE

He manages Olivia's household as a steward and has her trust because of the efficient execution of his duties. His grave, sober behavior is suited to Olivia's melancholy following her brother's death; he is desirable for curbing the activities of the irresponsible Sir Toby. He gains the servants' dislike for his severity, vanity, and the reports he carries to Olivia.

His official insignia is a chain of office and a cane. He dresses in black, the customary color of the Puritans, but he seems to wear, on occasion, flashy yellow stockings with cross-garters, which offer an excellent point for Maria's attack, because they are dear to his vanity, but do not match his stern and dignified bearing. We may imagine Malvolio to be a stately, rather florid man, with a moustache which he twirls importantly while speaking.

ABILITY

There is no doubt that Malvolio is a man of good intentions at first, and that he fulfills his position well. Olivia trusts him and thinks highly of him. He appears to be in her confidence to some extent, but he mistakes her trust for affection. His speech is precise and grave; his education is evidenced by his correct answers to Feste's questions on Pythagoras. His remark on Feste's wit shows observation, though it is exaggerated by his bitter critical nature.

MORALITY

Being a Puritan, Malvolio is strict and exacting in matters of morality. His honesty as a steward is beyond reproach; his complaints against Sir Toby's noisiness and drinking are justified, as is his objection to Maria's connivance at Sir Toby's requests for more wine.

HYPOCRISY

That Malvolio is a hypocrite is borne out by Maria's comment:

> The devil a puritan that he is, or anything constantly, but a
> time-pleaser (Act II, Sc. 3, 131)

He is a time-server who affects a standard of morality to which he does not always adhere. He is a good steward, but secretly aspires to the position of count, showing wordly ambition which is not in keeping with his air of dishonesty. He imagines himself living in luxury and wealth, "having come from a day-bed where I left Olivia sleeping" (Act II, Sc. 5, 44), and desires a good living which he scorns as a Puritan. His austerity is quite forgotten when he reads the letter which promises fulfillment of all his self-interested desires.

VANITY

Malvolio's vanity goes hand in hand with both his morality and hypocrisy. He displays his chain of office before others; he practises with his shadow when alone. He thinks that his smiles, frowns, grave speech, gaudy stockings and garters charm his mistress. He thinks that she loves him (Act II, Sc. 5, 20ff.) and that the servants and Sir Toby deserve to be treated with haughty condescension and harshness.

He has no doubt of his perfection, moral and otherwise. His conceit is his real vice, for his good qualities are so overrated by him that he is fooled by Maria's letter with the greatest ease, and he misjudges all that happens afterwards. His vanity robs him of all sense of humor; he magnifies his own virtues and the vices of others, and has no use for the harmless joking of Feste. Maria's letter cleverly exploits his vanity. It is broken by his imprisonment, for he humbly asks Feste to help him; but emerges again at the end when he shows how little he has learned by bitter experience.

SUPERIORITY

He is full of contempt for "Sir Toby and the lighter people." He speaks gravely and pompously, and refuses to enter into arguments with his supposed inferiors. His meetings with Viola are marked by haughtiness and insults; he throws the ring at her feet; he criticizes Olivia for being amused by Feste; he lectures Sir Toby like a school boy. He haughtily asks Olivia's explanation of the letter in Act V and does not apologize for blaming her for his maltreatment.

Fabian

He is introduced at an advanced stage of the plot, in Act II, Scene 5, and is a minor character. He has a grudge against Malvolio who "brought me out o' favour my lady over a bear-baiting here." He is less exuberant than Sir Toby, and tries hard to restrain him and Sir Andrew from betraying themselves while watching Malvolio from the bushes. He is fond of amusement, however, and helps Sir Toby in the arrangement of the duel, scaring Viola. He is afraid of Olivia's displeasure and has little part in Malvolio's imprisonment and maltreatment there. He asks Feste for Malvolio's letter, probably out of fear that it lays charges against him and the others. His defense of Maria and taking of the blame for Malvolio's baiting on himself and Sir Toby shows him to be courageous and to have a sense of responsibility.

Points of Interest

General Character of the Play

In general character, the play belongs to that section of Shakespeare's later comedy, which is usually characterized as joyous, refined and romantic. The other plays belonging to this section are *Much Ado About Nothing* and *As You Like It*, and with these, *Twelfth Night* has much in common. To quote Dr. Dowden:

> In the Later Comedies, again, it is quite remarkable how Shakespeare (generally in the portions of these plays which are due to his own invention) repeats with variations the incident of a trick or fraud practised upon one who is a self-lover, and its consequences, grave or gay . . . Malvolio is made an ass of by the mischievous Maria taking advantage of his solemn self-esteem; Beatrice and Benedick are cunningly entrapped, through their good-natured vanity, into love for which they had been already predisposed. . . . *Twelfth Night* resumes all the admirable humorous characteristics of the group of comedies which it completes. Then the change comes; *All's Well That Ends Well* is grave and earnest; *Measure for Measure* is dark and bitter.

Other resemblances between these plays will readily occur to those who are familiar with them. In *As You Like It*, as in *Twelfth Night*, the heroine appears in the dress of a man, in each one a girl falls in love with another, and each has its clown or fool, who wittily unmasks the follies of the others. The second name of the play, *What You Will*, is very like the name *As You Like It*.

Structure

There are two plots in *Twelfth Night*: the main plot is the love story, involving Olivia, Viola, Orsino, and, later on, Sebastian; the sub-plot is the conspiracy against Malvolio, involving the rest of the characters. It is a tribute to Shakespeare's genius that he was able to combine the two plots so effectively and credibly.

The introduction or exposition of the action is contained in Act I, which brings most of the chief characters except Sebastian on the stage, and starts the love triangle between Olivia, Viola and Orsino. Act II and part of Act III continue the second stage, the complication in both plots: Olivia's love for Viola complicates the main action; Malvolio is duped by Maria's letter, and disgraces himself before Olivia; and the duel between Sir Andrew and Viola is arranged. The climax, or crisis of the action is reached in Act III, Scene 4. Here, Antonio's entrance stops the duel and starts the series of confusions between the twins, giving Viola hope that her brother is alive. Act IV and part of the last act form the resolution or falling action; Sebastian is wedded to Olivia, Malvolio is humiliated in the cell, and the twins are further confused. The return of Sebastian in the last act constitutes the denouement, or the dramatic knot untied and brought to a conclusion by the double wedding announcements, the revelation of the conspiracy against Malvolio, and the return of the wounded Sir Toby and Sir Andrew. The play ends happily, except for Malvolio's vengeful exit.

Time in the Play

The action spans three days, with an interval of three days between the third and fourth scene of the first act. Viola comes to Illyria and to Orsino's court on the first day, while Valentine reports to Orsino on his errand to Olivia. Sir Toby and Sir Andrew have their first noisy revelry on that day also. In Scene 4 we are informed that Viola has been at Orsino's court for three days. Viola's mission to Olivia falls on the same day, and Sebastian is first introduced while the revenge on Malvolio is prepared by Sir Toby and Maria. All further action, from Act II, Scene 4 on, takes place on the third day. So much is crowded into the one day that we are not surprised by the Duke's statement that Viola has been with him three months (Act V, Sc. 1, 93).

Comic Scenes

The twelfth night after Christmas was the peak of the festive holiday season, and *Twelfth Night* is the peak of Shakespeare's festive days. It has five surefire comic scenes and an abundance of merriment: (1) the drinking bout of Sir Toby and his crony, abetted by Feste and Maria, and vainly protested by Malvolio (Uncounted comedies since have played variations upon this theme.); (2) the dropped letter, with Malvolio swallowing its suggestions hook, line, and sinker, while Sir Toby alternately rages and suppresses his mirth, behind the box tree; (3) the parade of Malvolio in his yellow stockings, before the supposedly melancholy Olivia; (4) the duel between the unwilling Viola and the equally reluctant Sir Andrew (This is, indeed, often overdone onstage; sometimes Viola surprises herself by beating Sir Andrew with the flat of her sword; sometimes Sir Andrew tries to avoid the blows by climbing up the scenery.); (5) the visit of Feste to Malvolio in the dark room, as the Fool pretends to be a curate and performs a dialogue in which he speaks both the part of the imaginary churchman and that of the Fool, before bringing pen and paper to the imprisoned Malvolio.

Malvolio

For the sake of this merry mood, we must be careful not to stress the affliction of Malvolio in the "dark room." To the Elizabethans, madness was a comic spectacle; Malvolio, "the cross-gartered gull." We must not make the mistake of the more sentimental among the Romantics and the moralistic Victorians, viewing the action of the play through the eyes of Olivia's steward.

Although Malvolio's manner was objectionable, and his self-love obnoxious, he was nonetheless carrying out Olivia's orders in seeking to restrain the boisterous excesses of Sir Toby and his companions. There is a basic decency in the steward and, despite his lack of humor, a virtue in his attitude that causes us to look beyond the surface to deeper significance within the play.

The Decaying Aristocracy

The characters are all of one social class, the rich aristocracy and its hangers-on. But in the exaggerated sentimentality of its leaders we may sense a whiff of decay, which grows stronger in the nostrils when we approach those of lesser rank. Maria, a young lady who should be learning gentle ways, is interested mainly in romping and low pranks. Sir Toby is the feudal retainer at his rowdy worst. Sir Andrew is the utter gentleman, thinned of his graces, reduced to a fool. In this aspect, *Twelfth Night* has been likened to Shaw's *Heartbreak House*, except that Shaw thumps his point home with a pile-driver, while Shakespeare lets you peep below the surface, so that you may smile or sigh — *What You Will*. And you may hope that the decaying aristocracy will be freshened and revitalized by the clear vision and decisive readiness of Viola and her twin.

Viola

Viola is, in truth, eager for reality. In every possible way, she gives expression to her love for Orsino, while loyally carrying out his orders to woo Olivia for him. She is forced into disguise, but the male masquerade bothers her. She is the character most aware, in this comedy, of the lack of awareness.

Audience's Viewpoint

The advantage of the audience at such a comedy is that we are completely aware. We match the deceived and the self-deceiving; we sort the understanding from the fools. Both Viola and Sebastian are at times bewildered, but neither is, in any important sense, deceived. Nor is the Fool, Feste, one of the fooled.

Artificial Melancholy in Main Plot

In the sphere of high comedy or, to put it another way, in the main plot, we are aware from the outset that Orsino and Olivia are self-deceived; they are caught in their separate patterns of sentimental self-indulgence. Orsino worships, idealizes, idolizes; he agonizes, at a distance, not over Olivia, but over an imaginary creature he confuses with Olivia. Olivia is borne, in equally sentimental self-indulgence, upon waves of melancholy, in her determination to preserve the memory of her brother — of whom, as a person, we are told nothing at all.

The artificiality of the melancholy indulged in by both Orsino and Olivia is brought to our attention in a number of ways. It is suggested by the deliberately exaggerated figures of speech in which he describes his longing and she her mournfulness, and in Orsino's restless shifting of his attention and desires. It is at times pointed out in explicit reference, as when Feste, leaving the Duke, exclaims, "Now, the melancholy god protect thee, and the tailor make thy doublet of changeable taffeta, for thy mind is a very opal." We have also observed, in the Notes, Feste's using Olivia's mourning to prove her a fool. And the artificiality of their mournful emotions is implicit in the contrast between Olivia and Orsino, and the twins whom they later marry. Viola, an orphan of the storm, virtually penniless, and a stranger to Illyria — and, in having a brother she believes lost, has as great cause for melancholy as Olivia — meets her situation with a direct drive to better it. Sebastian similarly takes opportunity by the horns. Although at the play's end Olivia calls Malvolio "poor fool," she earlier remarked, "I am as mad as he." Sebastian in his most bewildered moments can say " 'Tis wonder that enwraps me thus, yet 'tis not madness"; and again he makes an instant decision. Viola and Sebastian, in their steadiness and control, not only point up the defects of Orsino and Olivia, but, as the play progresses, seem competent to counterbalance the sentimentality of their future mates.

Subplot Parallels Main Plot

The sphere of low comedy, or the subplot, provides a comic criticism on the self-indulgence of the main characters. Contrasted to the constricted hothouse world of Orsino and Olivia is the ribald, sometimes crudely sensual world of Sir Toby Belch. Each world shows an excess that calls for balance with the other. And the exaggerated behavior of Orsino and Olivia has its opposite parallel in Sir Andrew Aguecheek, in whom it is reduced to absurdity, and in Malvolio, in whom it is soured by self-love. In their ways, these lowlier persons are as tangled in the unreality of excess as are the Duke and the lady. And while Malvolio is directly made to look the fool in his attempts to rise above his station, Sir Andrew goes home a poorer and sadder man, knowing he has been gulled. And Sir Toby — who devises the comic "punishment" of Malvolio and who gulls Sir Andrew — is himself repaid with a slight wound for his own excessive foolery.

Feste in Both Plots

It is Feste, the Fool, that moves, as even Viola does not, with equal ease in the world of low and high comedy. His mockery marks the line between affectation and sincerity. He helps us to evaluate the interrelated worlds of *Twelfth Night*; he helps to awaken the characters, so that we may share their enlightened understanding. And it is in Feste's terms that the play concludes, carrying us beyond the comedy to the world this side of the stage.

Levels of Reality in the Play

Note Fabian's comment, as Malvolio leaves to dress himself in yellow stockings and cross-garters, "If this were played upon a stage now, I could condemn it as an improbable fiction." This disarms us; we recognize and accept the fiction. We are reminded that not only Malvolio's dream is a fantasy, but all the movement of the play is a pretence. Thus the unravelling of the complications, with the recognition of the twin brother and sister, brings us back to reality — but only to the reality within the fiction, to the happy ending of lovers rightly matched forevermore. Then Feste, still with his muted music, which may make us smile or sigh, sings us to a gentle awareness of the world to which we must now return, when the Twelfth Night revelry gives way to "shut gates" and "drunken heads."

For most of the play, Orsino and Olivia live in their dream worlds apart, with Viola as the living bridge between them. Each of them fits her into the dream, until her true identity awakens them to reality. Then the ludicrous contrasts between folly and wisdom, melancholy and merriment, appearance and reality are incorporated into the final harmonies of marriage and music. This is the happy ending, with which the actors "strive to please you every day."

Use of Prose and Poetry

PROSE

Most of *Twelfth Night*, about two-thirds of the play, is in prose. Of the kinds and uses of prose, the following should be noted: (a) The prose style of the lower and comic characters, such as Sir Toby, Feste, Fabian and Malvolio; (b) the coloquial prose dialogue and matter-of-fact narrative in the scene of Sebastian and Antonio (Act II, Sc. 1); (c) the witty brilliant prose of high comedy, as in Viola's first meeting with Olivia (Act I, Sc. 5); (d) the prose of formal documents, as in Maria's letter, Sir Andrew's written challenge, and Malvolio's letter to Olivia.

POETRY

Roughly a third of the play is written in the blank verse measure; unrhymed iambic pentameter of ten syllables. *Twelfth Night* employs a flowing, graceful type of blank verse, typical of the "middle period" of

Shakespeare's art, less monotonous than the verse of earlier plays like *Richard III*, and more formal than the broken, majestically rushing blank verse of the late plays like *Macbeth*. The verse is flexible; it contains many run-on lines, incomplete lines, midline speech endings, and lines with irregular, non-iambic feet. Rhymed couplets occur repeatedly but less frequently than in the early plays of Shakespeare. They usually end a speech, or stress emotion (Viola's speech, Act III, Sc. 1, 155-160; Sebastian's speech, Act IV, Sc. 1, 59-62), or serve to make a generalized statement in epigram form (Antonio's words, Act III, Sc. 4, 343-346).

*The Masks of *Twelfth Night*

Love and its fulfillment are primary in Shakespeare's comedies. Its conflicts are often presented in terms of the battle of the generations. At the beginning of the plays the bliss of the young lovers is usually barred by an older generation of parents and rulers, a group which has supposedly experienced its own fulfillment in the past and which is now concerned with preserving old forms or fulfilling new ambitions. The comedies usually end with the triumph of young love, a triumph in which the lovers make peace with their elders and themselves assume adulthood and often power. The revolutionary force of love becomes an added element of vitality in a re-established society.

Twelfth Night does not follow the customary pattern. In this play the responsible older generation has been abolished, and there are no parents at all. In the first act we are rapidly introduced into a world in which the ruler is a love-sick Duke — in which young ladies, fatherless and motherless, embark on disguised actions, or rule, after a fashion, their own households, and in which the only individuals possibly over thirty are drunkards, jokesters, and gulls, totally without authority. All the external barriers to fulfillment have been eliminated in what becomes almost a parody of the state desired by the ordinary young lovers, the Hermias and Lysanders — or even the Rosalinds and Orlandos. According to the strictly romantic formula, the happy ending should be already achieved at the beginning of the play: we should abandon the theater for the rites of love. But the slightly stunned inhabitants of Illyria discover that they are anything but free. Their own actions provide the barriers, for most of them know neither themselves, nor others, nor their social world.

For his festival entertainment, Shakespeare freshly organized all the usual material of the romances — the twins, the exile, the impersonations — to provide significant movement for a dance of maskers. Every character has his mask, for the assumption of the play is that no one is without a mask in the serio-comic business of the pursuit of happiness. The character without disguises who is not ridiculous is outside the realm

* By Joseph H. Summers, from *The University Review*, XXII (Autumn, 1955).

of comedy. Within comedy, the character who thinks it is possible to live without assuming a mask is merely too naive to recognize the mask he has already assumed. He is the chief object of laughter. As a general rule, we laugh with the characters who know the role they are playing and we laugh at those who do not; we can crudely divide the cast of *Twelfth Night* into those two categories.

But matters are more complicated than this, and roles have a way of shifting. All the butts except perhaps Sir Andrew Aguecheek have moments in which they are the masters of our laughter; yet all the masters have moments in which they appear as fools. In our proper confusion, we must remember the alternative title of the play, "What You Will." It may indicate that everyone is free to invent his own title for the proceedings. It also tells the author's intention to fulfill our desires: we wish to share in the triumphs of love and we wish to laugh; we wish our fools occasionally to be wise, and we are insistent that our wisest dramatic figures experience our common fallibility. Most significantly, the title may hint that what "we" collectively "will" creates all the comic masks — that society determines the forms of comedy more directly than it determines those of any other literary genre.

At the opening of the play Orsino and Olivia accept the aristocratic (and literary) ideas of the romantic lover and the grief-stricken lady as realities rather than as ideas. They are comic characters exactly because of that confusion. Orsino glories in the proper moodiness and fickleness of the literary lover; only our own romanticism can blind us to the absurdities in his opening speech. Orsino first wishes the music to continue so that the appetite of love may "surfeit"; immediately, however, he demands that the musicians stop the music they are playing to repeat an isolated phrase — an awkward procedure and a comic bit of stage business which is rarely utilized in productions. Four lines later the music must stop entirely because the repeated "strain" no longer *is* sweet, and the appetite is truly about to "surfeit." He then exclaims that the spirit of love is so "quick and fresh" that like the sea (hardly a model of freshness)

> naught enters there,
> Of what validity and pitch soe'er,
> But falls into abatement and low price,
> Even in a minute!

Orsino is a victim of a type of madness to which the most admirable characters are sometimes subject. Its usual causes are boredom, lack of physical love, and excessive imagination, and the victim is unaware that he is in love with love rather than with a person.

In the same scene, before we ever see the lady, Olivia's state is as nicely defined. Valentine, Orsino's messenger, has acquired something of his master's extraordinary language, and his report on his love mission manages both to please the Duke and to convey his own incredulity at the excess of Olivia's vow for her brother. In his speech the fresh and the salt are again confused. It is impossible to keep fresh something so ephemeral as grief; Olivia can make it last and "season" it, however, by the process of pickling — the natural effect of "eye-offending brine." Orsino feels unbounded admiration for the depth of soul indicated by Olivia's vow and at the same time he assumes that the vow can easily be broken by a lover. He departs for "sweet *beds* of flow'rs" which are somehow to provide a *canopy* for "love-thoughts."

Both Orsino and Olivia have adopted currently fashionable literary postures; yet neither of them is a fool. We are glad to be reassured by the Captain that Orsino is "A noble duke, in nature as in name," and that his present infatuation is only a month old. Sir Toby's later remark "What a plague means my niece, to take the death of her brother thus?" indicates that Olivia too had seemed an unlikely candidate for affectation. She is also an unconvincing practitioner. Although at our first glimpse of her she is properly the grief-stricken lady ("Take the fool away"), her propriety collapses under Feste's famous catechism. We discover that Olivia is already bored and that she really desires to love. Outraged nature has its full and comic revenge when Olivia falls passionately in love with a male exterior and acts with an aggressiveness which makes Orsino seem almost feminine. Still properly an actor in comedy, Olivia quickly changes from the character who has confused herself with a socially attractive mask to one who fails to perceive the mask which society has imposed on another.

Viola's situation allows time for neither love- nor grief-in-idleness. A virgin, shipwrecked in a strange land, possessing only wit and intelligence and the Captain's friendship, she must act immediately if she is to preserve herself. She, like Olivia, has "lost" a brother, but the luxury of conventional mourning is quickly exchanged for a *willed* hope that, as she was saved, "so perchance may he be." With Viola's wish for time to know what her "estate is," before she is "delivered to the world," we are reminded that society often requires a mask, neither for the relief of boredom nor the enjoyment of acting, but merely for self-preservation. While Antonio, "friend to Sebastian," almost loses his life because of his failure to assume a disguise, Viola suffers from no failure of discretion or imagination. She must assume a disguise as a boy and she must have help in preparing it.

Although she knows the ways of the world, Viola takes the necessary chance and wills to trust the Captain:

> There is a fair behavior in thee, Captain.
> And though that Nature with a beauteous wall
> Doth oft close in pollution, yet of thee
> I will believe thou hast a mind that suits
> With this thy fair and outward character.

We have in this second scene not only the beginning of one strand of the complicated intrigue, but also the creation of the one character active in the intrigue who provides a measure for the comic excessess of all the others. (Feste's role as observer is analogous to Viola's role as "actor.") Although Viola chooses to impersonate Cesario from necessity, she later plays her part with undisguised enjoyment. She misses none of the opportunities for parody, for confession, and for *double entendre* which the mask affords, and she never forgets or lets us forget the biological distance between Viola and Cesario. Except in the fencing match with Sir Andrew Aguecheek, she anticipates and directs our perception of the ludicrous in her own role as well as in the roles of Orsino and Olivia.

Sebastian is the reality of which Cesario is the artful imitation. Viola's twin assumes no disguises; Viola and the inhabitants of Illyria have assumed it for him. He is, to the eye, identical with Viola, and his early scenes with Antonio serve to remind us firmly of his existence as well as to introduce an initial exhilarating confusion at the entrance of either of the twins. When he truly enters the action of the play in Act IV he is certainly the object of our laughter, not because he has confused himself with an ideal or improper mask, but because he so righteously and ineffectually insists on his own identity in the face of unanimous public opposition. Our attitude quickly changes, however, to a mixture of amused patronization and identification: we do, after all, *know* so much more than does Sebastian; yet, within the context of the play, we can hardly keep from identifying with the gentleman who, practically if not idealistically, decides not to reject the reality of a passionate Olivia just because he has never seen her before:

> Or I am mad, or else this is a dream.
> Let fancy still my sense in Lethe steep.
> If it be thus to dream, still let me sleep!

The other characters in the play do not truly belong to an aristocracy of taste and leisure. For some of them, that is the chief problem. Malvolio and Sir Andrew Aguecheek are ruled by their mistaken notions of the proper role of an upper-class gentleman, and they fail to perceive the comic gaps between themselves and their ideal roles, and between those ideals and the social reality. Sick with self-love as he is, Malvolio is also sick with his desire to rise in society: "an affectioned ass, that cons state without book and utters it by great swaths: the best persuaded of himself, so crammed, as he thinks, with excellencies, that it is his grounds of faith that all look on him love him." Although he knows it without, he has learned his "state" by book — but such a pupil inevitably distorts the text. He dreams of ruling a thrifty and solemn household while he plays with "some rich jewel," a dream characteristically attractive to the *arriviste* and absolutely impossible to the *arrive*. We, like Maria, "can hardly forbear hurling things at him." He is as absurd as the reverse image which possesses Sir Andrew, a carpet-knight rightly described by Sir Toby as "an ass-head and a coxcomb and a knave, a thin-faced knave, a gull!" In the gallery of false images Sir Andrew's roaring boy hangs opposite Malvolio's burgher. Although in a low moment Sir Andrew may think that he has "no more wit than a Christian or an ordinary man has," he never has such grave self-doubt for long. Like a true gull, he tries to assume the particular role which, of all others, he is most poorly equipped to play: drinker, fighter, wencher.

Sir Andrew, however, would hardly exist without Sir Toby Belch: the full must have his guller. Sir Toby may fulfill Sir Andrew's idea of what a gentleman should be, but Sir Toby himself has no such odd idea of gentility. (Sir Andrew may be "a dear manikin to you, Sir Toby," but Sir Toby has a superlatively good reason for allowing him to be: "I have been dear to him, lad, some two thousand strong, or so.") Even at his most drunken, we are delightfully unsure whether we laugh at or with Sir Toby, whether he is or is not fully conscious of the effects as well as the causes of his "mistakes," his verbal confusions, and even his belches. Like another drunken knight, and like Viola, Toby possesses a range of dramatic talents and he enjoys using them. He is equally effective as the fearless man of action, as the practioner of noble "gentleness" with the "mad" Malvolio, and as the experienced alcoholic guide to Sir Andrew. His joy is in the jest as well as in the bottle, and he can bring himself to abandon the latter long enough to marry Maria simply in admiration for her ability as an intriguer. But like other knowing players, Sir Toby is vulnerable to deception. He is object rather than master of our laughter from the time when he mistakes Sebastian for Cesario and attempts to assert his masculine ability as a swordsman.

In the business of masking, Feste is the one professional among a crowd of amateurs; he does it for a living. He never makes the amateur's mistake of confusing his personality with his mask — he wears not motley in his brain. Viola recognizes his wisdom and some kinship in the fact that each "must observe their mood on whom he jests." But though Feste may have deliberately chosen his role, society determines its conditions. Now that he is growing old, the conditions become difficult: "Go to, you're a dry fool, I'll no more of you. Besides, you grow dishonest." While all the other characters are concerned with gaining something they do not have, Feste's struggle is to retain his mask and to make it again ingratiating. He is able to penetrate all the masks of the others, and he succeeds in retaining his own.

However fanciful its dreams of desire, the play moves within a context of an almost real world, from one disguise and half-understood intrigue to another, until all its elements are whirled into a complexly related and moving figure. With the constant contrasts and parallels and reversals in character, situation, and intrigue, we find ourselves at last, along with Malvolio and Olivia and Viola and the rest, in a state of real delirium. Until the concluding scene, however, we can largely agree with Sebastian: if we dream, we do not wish to wake; if this is madness, it is still comic madness, and we do not envy the sane. The attempts at false and inflexible authority are being defeated, the pretentious are being deflated, and the very sentimentality of the likable sentimentalists has led them close to biological reality. We are particularly delighted with Viola. Young, intelligent, zestful, she is a realist. She cuts through the subterfuges and disguises of the others with absolute clarity, and she provides us with a center for the movement, a standard of normality which is never dull. In her rejection of the artificial myths of love, moreover, Viola never becomes the advocate of a far more terrifying myth, the myth of absolute rationality. In a completely rational world, Shakespeare never tires of pointing out, what we know as love could not exist. We have never desired such a world.

From the time of her first aside to the audience after she has seen Orsino ("Yet a barful strife!/Whoe'er I woo, myself would be his wife"), Viola directly admits her irrational love. She differs, then, from Orsino and Olivia not in any invulnerability to blindness and passion, but in the clarity and simplicity with which she recognizes and accepts her state. Reason is not abandoned: she rationally admits her irrationality and her inability to cope with the situation:

> O Time, thou must untangle this, not I!
> It is too hard a knot for me to untie!

Viola needs a miracle. Although she may imagine herself as "Patience on a monument, smiling at grief," she remains as close as possible to her loved one and waits for the miracle to happen. Since we have seen Sebastian, we know that the miracle will occur; yet through our identification with Viola we come to know the comic burden, the masker's increasing weariness of the mask which implies that love is still pursued rather than possessed.

The burden becomes comically unbearable only in the final scene, when it is cast off. Here Shakespeare underscores all those possibilities of violence and death which are usually submerged in comedy. Antonio is arrested and in danger of his life. Orsino, finally recognizing the hopelessness of his suit to Olivia, shows the vicious side of sentimentality. After considering the possibility of killing Olivia "like to the Egyptian thief," he determines to do violence to "Cesario":

> Come, boy, with me. My thoughts are ripe in mischief.
> I'll sacrifice the lamb that I do love,
> To spite a raven's heart within a dove.

Olivia is hysterical at what seems to be the baseness of Cesario. Sir Toby has a broken pate to show for his one major failure to penetrate a mask. The dance must stop. The miracle must occur.

The entrance of Sebastian is "what we will." It is the most dramatic moment of the play. The confrontation of Sebastian and Cesario-Viola, those identical images, concludes the formal plot and provides the means for the discarding of all the lovers' masks. The moment must be savored and fully realized. As Viola and Sebastian chant their traditional formulas of proof, both the audience and the other characters on the stage undistractedly view the physical image of the duality which has made the confusion and the play. The masks and the play are to be abandoned for a vision of delight beyond delight, in which lovers have neither to wear nor to penetrate disguises since they are at last invulnerable to error and laughter.

Yet the play does not resolve into a magic blessing of the world's fertility as does *A Midsummer Night's Dream*. We have been promised a happy ending, and we receive it. We are grateful that the proper Jacks and Jills have found each other, but the miracle is a limited miracle, available only to the young and the lucky. Not every Jack has his Jill even in Illyria, and after the general unmasking, those without love may seem even lonelier. Malvolio, of course, is justly punished. He has earned his mad scene, and with the aid of Feste he has made it comic. As a result of his humiliation he has also earned some sort of redress. Yet he is ridiculous in his arrogance to the end, and his threatened revenge, now that he is powerless to effect it, sustains the comedy and the characterization and prevents the obtrusion of destructive pathos.

It is Feste rather than Malvolio who finally reminds us of the limitations and the costs of the romantic vision of happiness with which we have been seduced. However burdensome, masking is his career, and romantic love provides no end for it. Alone on the stage at the end of the play, he sings a song of unfulfilled love which shows the other side of the coin. For Feste, as for his audience, the mask can never be finally discarded: the rain it raineth every day. His song has those overtones, I believe, but they are only overtones. The music, here and elsewhere in the play, provides an element in which oppositions may be resolved. And the song itself, like the movement which must accompany it, is crude and witty as well as graceful and nostalgic. However far it may have missed the conventionally happy ending, Feste's saga of misfortunes in love is comic, even from his own point of view. The exaggeration so often operative in the refrains of Elizabethan lyrics emphasizes that the watery as well as the sunny vision can become funny: it doesn't rain every day by a long shot.

The song, which begins as the wittiest observer's comment on the denouement of the play, ends as a dissolution of the dramatic fiction:

> A great while ago the world begun,
>> With hey, ho, the wind and the rain,
> But that's all one, our play is done,
>> And we'll strive to please you every day.

The audience has been a participant in the festivity. As the fictional lovers have unmasked to reveal or realize their "true" identities, it is only proper that the clown, the only character who might move freely in the environs of Bankside, as well as in the realm of Illyria, should unmask the whole proceeding for the imitation of a desired world which it has been. The audience must be returned from "What You Will" to its own less patterned world where the sea rarely disgorges siblings given up for lost, where mistaken marriages rarely turn out well, where Violas rarely catch Dukes, and where Malvolios too often rule households with disturbing propriety. The lovers have met, and Feste announces that present laughter has come to an end. But the actors, those true and untiring maskers, will continue to "strive to please" us. They will find few occasions in the future in which their efforts will be more sure of success.

Twelfth Night is the climax of Shakespeare's early achievement in comedy. The effects and values of the earlier comedies are here subtly embodied in the most complex structure which Shakespeare had yet created. But the play also looks forward: the pressure to dissolve the comedy, to realize and finally abandon the burden of laughter, is an intrinsic part of its "perfection." Viola's clear-eyed and affirmative vision of her own and the world's irrationality is a triumph and we desire it; yet we realize its vulnerability, and we come to realize that virtue in disguise is only totally triumphant when evil is not in disguise — is not truly present at all. Having solved magnificently the problems of this particular form of comedy, Shakespeare was evidently not tempted to repeat his triumph. After Twelfth Night the so-called comedies require for their happy resolutions more radical characters and devices — omniscient and omnipresent Dukes, magic, and resurrection. More obvious miracles are need for comedy to exist in a world in which evil also exists, not merely incipiently but with power.

Selected Criticisms

The love of Viola is the sweetest and tenderest emotion that ever informed the heart of the purest and the most graceful of beings, with a spirit almost divine. Perhaps in the whole range of Shakespeare's poetry there is nothing which comes more unbidden into the mind, and always in connexion with some image of the ethereal beauty of the utterer, than Viola's celebrated speech to the Duke in her assumed garb of the page.

Charles Cowden Clarke

Of all Shakespeare's Comedies, perhaps Twelfth Night is the most richly woven with various hues of love, serious and mock-heroic. The amorous threads take warmer shifting colours from their neighbourhood to the unmitigated remorseless merry-making of the harum-scarum old wag Sir Toby and his sparkling captain in mischief, the "most excellent devil of wit," Maria. Beside their loud conviviality and pitiless fun the languishing sentiment of the cultivated love-lorn Duke stands out seven times refined, and goes with exquisite touch to the innermost sensibilities.

William Minto

Many of the conflicts of *Twelfth Night* seem to be concerned with the contest between human will and suprahuman control; yet, the latter manifests itself in various ways and is called different names by the characters themselves. As each contest between the human will and another designer works itself out, the involved characters recognize that their will is fulfilled, but not according to their planning. The individual's will is finally secondary to a design that benevolently, but unpredictably, accords with what he truly desires. For example, when Olivia, at the end of Act I, implores Fate to accord with her will in allowing her love for Cesario to flourish, she has no idea that her will must be circumvented for her own happiness. Yet the substitution of Sebastian for Cesario in her love fulfills her wishes more appropriately than her own design could have done . . .

The playwright, like the comic providence in the play, has understood "what we will" and has led us to a pleasurable fulfillment of our desires, but in ways which we could not have foreseeen or controlled. The substitution of the final line, "And we'll strive to please you every day," for the refrain, "For the rain it raineth every day," is a crucial change. Like the incremental repetition in the folk ballad, this pessimistic refrain has built a dynamic tension which is released in the recognition that the play is an actual experience in the lives of the audience, even though it is enacted in an imagined world. The players, and the playwright who arranges them, are engaged in an ongoing effort to please the audience. The providential design remains incomplete within the play's action and only promises a "golden time"; similarly, the playwright promises further delightful experiences for his audience. The subplot's action, on the other hand, is limited within the framework of revenge; the revenge of the subplot characters elicits Malvolio's cry for revenge.

Malvolio is the only one who refuses to see himself in a subservient position to a larger design. And possibly because that design is too small, we cannot feel that his abuse and final exclusion from the happy community of lovers and friends allows the golden time to be fulfilled within the play. Feste's manipulation of Malvolio resembles the playwright's manipulation of his audience's will, but in such a reduced way that we cannot avoid seeing the difference between merely human revenge and the larger benevolence that controls the play's design.

Joan Hartwig

Twelfth Night, the latest of the great trio of romantic comedies, is in some ways the most delightful. In its blend of romance and realism, sentiment and fun, its well-knit construction, vigorous characterization, and happy balance of lovely verse and lively prose, it is certainly the most finished of Shakespeare's comedies. And it is characteristic of Shakespeare's development and of his method of work that he never thereafter wrote a comedy like this. It has been called 'Shakespeare's farewell to mirth.' This is hardly accurate; there are comic characters, merry scenes, and hearty laughs in his latest plays, *The Winter's Tale* and *The Tempest*; yet there is never again a comedy which in all-round perfection can compare with *Twelfth Night* . . .

The action in *Twelfth Night* is lively and varied enough to hold the attention even of a reluctant audience. In the main plot there is always the interest aroused by a well-knit intrigue, growing more complicated till the deft solution at the very end. It differs in this from *Much Ado*, in which, after the effective church scene, the interest begins to flag, since it has already been made clear that Hero will be saved. It is incomparably better in this respect than *As You Like It*, in which, strictly speaking, there is no intrigue at all. Long before that play was over, the end must have been evident to any intelligent auditor. There is, to be sure, little of broad comedy in the closing scenes of *Twelfth Night*. An exception might, perhaps, be made for the scene of the duel, in which Viola is reluctantly involved. Properly acted, however, this scene should not be allowed to sink into farce. Viola's reluctance is characteristic of her femininity, but she does accurately draw her sword and prepare for combat rather than disclose the secret of her sex. She would not reveal it to the man she loves, still less to the bullies who have thrust a quarrel on her. Her rescue at the critical moment by Antonio is an ingenious stroke of Shakespeare's art; he found nothing like it in any of the versions he may have glanced at; in fact the whole scene is Shakespeare's invention. In the main what we have of comedy in the romantic action is the comedy of sentiment and situation: the disguised heroine acting as a messenger for her beloved to the lady he loves and her own involvement in the lady's sudden passion for her. This is the motif already employed in *The Two Gentlemen*, but it is far more fully and sensitively developed here.

It is a different matter with the underplot. Here there is plenty of comic action, from Sir Andrew's capers in his first scene to the midnight revel and the mockery of the imprisoned Malvolio. Yet anything like the old horseplay is avoided in this refined comedy. After a brief exchange of buffets the threatened fight between Sebastian and Sir Toby is stopped by Olivia's appearance and her rebuke of her ungracious uncle. A scene in which Sebastian breaks the heads of the two knights is reported, but carefully kept off-stage. The comedy of the underplot is mainly a matter of situation, as in the repeated instances of mistaken identity and in Malvolio's interpretation of the forged letter accompanied by the mocking comments of his unseen hearers. Sometimes it is simply a matter of words, as in Feste's catechism of his mistress and Malvolio's daydream before he finds the letter.   Thomas Marc Parrott

This is justly considered as one of the most delightful of Shakespear's comedies. It is full of sweetness and pleasantry. It is perhaps too good-natured for comedy. It has little satire, and no spleen. It aims at the ludicrous rather than the ridiculous. It makes us laugh at the follies of mankind, not despise them, and still less bear any ill-will towards them. Shakespear's comic genius resembles the bee rather in its power of extracting sweets from weeds or poisons, than in leaving a sting behind it. He gives the most amusing exaggeration of the prevailing foibles of his characters, but in a way that they themselves, instead of being offended at, would almost join in to humour; he rather contrives opportunities for them to shew themselves off in the happiest lights, than renders them contemptible in the perverse construction of the wit or malice of others.

There is a certain stage of society in which people become conscious of their peculiarities and absurdities, affect to disguise what they are, and set up pretensions to what they are not. This gives rise to a corresponding style of comedy, the object of which is to detect the disguises of self-love, and to make reprisals on these preposterous assumptions of vanity, by marking the contrast between the real and the affected character as severely as possible, and denying to those, who would impose on us for what they are not, even the merit which they have. This is the comedy of artificial life, of wit and satire, such as we see it in Congreve, Wycherley, Vanbrugh, &c. To this succeeds a state of society from which the same sort of affectation and pretence are banished by a greater knowledge of the world or by their successful exposure on the stage; and which by neutralising the materials of comic character, both natural and artificial, leaves no comedy at all — but *the sentimental*. Such is our modern comedy. There is a period in the progress of manners anterior to both these, in which the foibles and follies of individuals are of nature's planting, not the growth of art or study; in which they are therefore unconscious of them themselves, or care not who knows them, if they can but have their whim out; and in which, as there is no attempt at imposition, the spectators rather receive pleasure from humouring the inclinations of the persons they laugh at, than wish to give them pain by exposing their absurdity. This may be called the comedy of nature, and it is the comedy which we generally find in Shakespear.

Whether the analysis here given be just or not, the spirit of his comedies is evidently quite distinct from that of the authors above mentioned, as it is in its essence the same with that of Cervantes, and also very frequently of Moliere, though he was more systematic in his extravagance than Shakespear. Shakespear's comedy is of a pastoral and poetical cast. Folly is indigenous to the soil, and shoots out with native, happy, unchecked luxuriance. Absurdity has every encouragement afforded it; and nonsense has room to flourish in. . . .

The great and secret charm of *Twelfth Night* is the character of Viola. Much as we like catches and cakes and ale, there is something that we like better. We have a friendship for Sir Toby; we patronise Sir Andrew; we have an understanding with the Clown, a sneaking kindness for Maria and her rogueries; we feel a regard for Malvolio, and sympathise with his gravity, his smiles, his cross garters, his yellow stockings, and imprisonment in the stocks. But there is something that excites in us a stronger feeling than all this — it is Viola's confession of her love.

> *Duke.*   What's her history?
> *Viola.*   *A blank, my lord, she never told her love.*
> She let concealment, like a worm i' th' bud,
> Feed on her damask cheek: she pin'd in thought,
> And with a green and yellow melancholy,
> She sat like Patience on a monument,
> Smiling at grief. *Was not this love indeed?*
> We men may say more, swear more, but indeed,
> Our shews are more than will; for still we prove
> Much in our vows, but little in our love.
> *Duke.*   But died thy sister of her love, my boy?
> *Viola.*   I am all the daughters of my father's house,
> And all the brothers too; — and yet I know not.

William Hazlitt

. . . What then is folly and what wisdom, the comedy seems to ask. The question first appeared in that early cross-talk with the fool which brought Olivia into contrast with Malvolio even while we were awaiting her reception of Cesario. So that the manner in which Malvolio's story is begun clearly puts it into relation with the main plot of the wooing. And of course it is only appropriate that scenes of romantic love should be surrounded by a comic dialogue which gaily tosses off its hints about whether these characters are fools. For the pursuit of the ideal life is not quite compatible with reason. And, as another of Shakespeare's comedies puts it, those who in imagination see more than "reason ever comprehends" are the lover, the poet, and the lunatic. So where does the noble vision end and the madman's dream begin? The greatness and the folly that lie in the mind of man are inextricably entangled and the characters in *Twelfth Night* have each their share of both. Malvolio's moment of lunacy may be, as Lamb suggests, the moment of his glory. Yet Malvolio, so scornful of the follies of others, would persuade us that his own are sane. His sanity is indeed established, but only to leave us wondering whether sanity may not sometimes be the greater folly. What the comedy *may* suggest is that he who in his egotism seeks to fit the world to the procrustean bed of his own reason deserves his own discomfiture. But Olivia, who self-confessedly abandons reason, and Orsino, who avidly gives his mind to all the shapes of fancy, are permitted to pass through whatever folly there may be in this to a greater illumination. Although what they sought has inevitably eluded them, it has nevertheless been vouchsafed to them in another form.

Yet it is the art of Shakespeare's comedy, and perhaps also its wisdom, to make no final judgments. The spirit of the piece, after all, is that of Twelfth Night and it is in the ideal world of Twelfth Night that Malvolio may be justly punished. Perhaps we should also remember, as even the Twelfth Night lovers do, to pause, if only for a moment, to recognize his precisian virtues. Olivia agrees with him that he has been "notoriously abused" and the poet-lover Orsino sends after him to "entreat him to a peace," before they finally enter into the happiness to which "golden time" will summon them. "Golden time" — the epithet is characteristically Orsino's. It is only the wise fool who stays to sing to us about the rain that raineth every day.

Harold Jenkins

Twelfth Night, first mentioned in Manningham's *Diary* on February 2, 1601-2, is often regarded as Shakespeare's most perfect comedy. It is certainly a drama of very careful workmanship. It has behind it a complexity of slightly differing sources which have been carefully fused together. Like *The Merchant of Venice* it has something allegorical to say about the nature of true love, and like *As You Like It* it has a great clown. An added feature is an episode in contemporary satire in which Shakespeare ridicules and punishes an upstart servant, Malvolio. The spectacle of the over-ambitious servant aspiring beyond his station was no doubt abominable in the eyes of the Elizabethan upper-classes; and here again, as in *The Merchant of Venice*, a change in social sentiment has caused even great actors to distort the comedy by making Malvolio unpleasantly threatening, if not actually tragic.

Twelfth Night is indeed excellent in workmanship — in plot and minor plot, liveliness and variety of incident, and sharply drawn characters. Structurally it is a joy. No wonder it has been singled out as Shakespeare's most perfect comedy. Those who have so regarded it have usually had in mind, not only that Shakespeare has outdone himself, but that in *Twelfth Night* he has approached most nearly the hard and glittering objectivity of Latin comedy, and of Jonson, Molière, and Congreve. The so-called pure comedy of these worthies, much admired, refuses to have pity for folly, or even for misfortune of a sort. It takes no sides in the issue between the rogue and his dupe. It likes the spectacle of the biter bit, but it also adds "the rod for the fool's back." The idea that *Twelfth Night* is Shakespeare's nearest approach to the comedy of wit and the comedy of spectacle is attractive enough; and yet, for all that, *Twelfth Night* is a romantic comedy. The impression of its detachment arises in part from the fact that it is the most realistic of Shakespeare's Italianate comedies. This comedy of romance and ideal love is played against a background of what many believe was a familiar upper-class English household, that of the Lady Olivia, with some contributions from the Duke's *ménage*. There are also two sea captains, both of an honest, kindly type perhaps not unfamiliar on the streets of London.

The steward, Malvolio, was Shakespeare's nemesis in pure comedy.

His very name seems to indicate that Shakespeare regarded him as an ill-natured person, and he is. Malvolio is a precisian — Shakespeare refuses to call him a Puritan — a precisian not from scrupulous morals but from jealousy of the pastimes of others. Sir Toby hits him and his kind off to the world's satisfaction when he says, "Dost thou think, because thou art virtuous, there shall be no more cakes and ale." In his capacity as a steward Malvolio is not without dignity (of a self-conceited kind), responsibility, and usefulness, so that the Lady Olivia says she would not have him miscarry for half her dowry, but it is she who tells him he is "sick of self-love." He is a prig and belongs to the well-hated class of upper-servants who persecute their inferiors and seek to extend their authority into fields where it has no necessity or propriety. He is called an "affection'd [or affected] ass," and his exaggerated superior bearing offers opportunity for caricature.

Hardin Craig

Review Questions and Answers

Question 1.

Assuming that the opening speech often furnishes a clue to the nature of the whole play, what would you expect to be the character of *Twelfth Night*.

Answer

Music and love are the themes of the Duke's first speech. These are conceived and spoken of in a poetic and imaginative spirit, suggesting that they have been made the objects of an absorbing and enchanting study rather than that the Duke is completely swayed and mastered by deep passion. Hence, we expect, and rightly so, that love is to be the theme of the drama, and that the love will be treated poetically and somewhat playfully. In other words, we are led to believe that the play will be a romantic comedy, rather than a tragedy of passion.

Question 2.

In which of Shakespeare's other plays are girls disguised as boys?

Answer

To make the heroine (or other female characters) of a drama assume male attire was a favorite effect of the stage in Shakespeare's time, and one to which the custom of boys acting the female parts invited. But Shakespeare was never led into the error of making his disguised boys appear overly masculine. On the contrary, they all resemble one another in that, as Dowden remarks, they are "the most impulsively or the most delicately and exquisitely feminine of his women."

The following are the names of Shakespeare's women who assume male disguise, together with the names of the plays in which they play their parts.

Two Gentlemen of Verona: **Julia** is in love with Proteus. When Proteus parts from her, she follows him, disguised as a boy. Finding him in love with another girl, Silvia, Julia (disguised as Sebastian) becomes Proteus' servant. As with Viola, the play ends happily for Julia.

The Merchant of Venice: **Portia** is wealthy, wise, witty, and more intelligent than most of Shakespeare's other female characters. In order to rescue her lover's friend, Antonio, from the powerful Shylock, she disguises herself as a lawyer. She conducts Antonio's defence brilliantly, and wins the case.

Nerissa, in the same play, is the friend and waiting-maid of Portia. She acts as a lawyer's clerk in the great judgment scene.

Jessica, again in the same play, is Shylock's daughter. Hating her home and ashamed of her father, she disguises herself as a boy and elopes with Lorenzo.

As You Like It: **Rosalind** is the daughter of a banished Duke, and the play's delightful and witty heroine. She enjoys her disguise and throws herself into her part with more zest than Viola, and consequently, plays the role even better.

Cymbeline: **Imogen** has fallen from favor by marrying Posthamus Leonatas, a 'poor but worthy gentleman'. She disguises herself as a boy, Fidele, to escape from a plot to kill her. She is more sincere and simple than Portia, and more fully characterized than Rosalind or Viola.

Question 3.

Discuss the theme of self-love in *Twelfth Night*.

Answer

Self-love or egotism comes in many different forms. For some, it manifests itself as vanity and ambitiousness; for others, it appears as selfishness, self-absorption or pride. What characterizes all forms of self-love is the belief that one is superior or more important than anyone else, and this is the basic fault of almost every character in *Twelfth Night*, with the possible exceptions of Viola, Sebastian, Antonio and Fabian.

What makes Malvolio, Olivia's trusted and valued steward, comical is not the fact that he is a fool; it is his self-conceit. He mistakes the high opinion his mistress has of him, and the favor she has shown him for genuine affection. This leads him to believe that he has a chance of being Olivia's husband, and it is on this that Maria devises her plan to humiliate him. Thus, it is his self-love which is responsible for his downfall.

Olivia, regardless of her other good qualities, is driven by self-love. While we do not condemn her for grieving for her brother, her grief does seem exaggerated, especially when we compare it with Viola's. This exaggerated grief appears to be based on an egotistical desire for self-dramatization and self-pity. Further, she displays great pride in the way that she treats Orsino. She knows how strongly he feels for her, yet she is cold and unsympathetic. In her attempts to win 'Cesario' (Viola), despite what he (she) seems to feel, Olivia appears selfish. This applies equally well to Orsino: he too is "sick of self-love". He is so completely self-absorbed in love-melancholy that he actually seems to enjoy his misery. The Duke is a perfect example of someone who is more in love with love than with a particular person. He learns a truer, less sentimental love from Viola.

Vanity is the form that Sir Andrew Aguecheek's self-love takes. He was vain to even think that he stood a chance of winning Olivia's affection, and it was because of his vanity that Sir Toby was so easily able to manipulate him.

Sir Toby's and Maria's self-love manifests itself in the forms of self-absorption and selfishness. Sir Toby's desire to manipulate and swindle Sir Andrew, his gluttony and drunkenness, and the tremendous enjoyment he derives from seeing Malvolio humiliated all point to his overwhelming egotism. Maria's plots to win Sir Andrew and put Malvolio in his place, and her self-confidence make her a perfect match for Sir Andrew in all respects. Even Feste suffers from self-love. It was not merely professional pride that made him so angry at Malvolio's insults; it was conceit and egotism which drove him to take such pleasure in Malvolio's misfortune.

Question 4.

Discuss the propriety of Shakespeare's use of puns, and give some examples from this play.

Answer

It is the custom in this age of refinement in which we live to condemn puns as being 'in bad taste.' They are said to be 'unnatural,' the 'cheapest form of wit,' 'vulgar' and so on. But we must not allow ourselves to forget that there are fashions in speech as there are in dress, and that what is considered correct in one age is denounced in another. Coleridge defended Shakespeare's use of puns on the ground that "the dramatist represents his characters in every situation of life, and in every state of mind, and there is no form of language that may not be introduced with effect by a great and judicious poet, and yet be strictly according to nature." The use of puns in a comedy may be indicated as belonging to the "state, age, feeling of the individual" from whose mouth they are made to proceed; in a tragedy or serious play the practice may be justified as belonging to the age in which the poet lived. "In a certain degree," says Ulrici, "play of words is the appropriate and most natural form of the comic in detail, as also it is unquestionably the most original vehicle of wit." Examples in the play are numerous and will be found to proceed for the most part from the comic characters Maria, Toby, and the Clown, who describes himself as Lady Olivia's "corrupter of words."

The following list contains some of the more important examples: On *exceptions* and *except* (Act I, Sc. 3, 6-7); on *confine* and *finer* (Act I, Sc. 3, 10); on two meanings of *natural* (Act I, Sc. 3, 30); on two meanings of *dry* (Act I, Sc. 3, 78-81); on two meanings of *put down* (Act I, Sc. 3, 88-90); on *tongs* and *tongues* (Act I, Sc. 3, 99-107); on two meanings of *caper* (Act I, Sc. 3, 131); on two meanings of *points* (Act I, Sc. 5, 26); on two meanings of *salt water* (Act II, Sc. 1, 32-3); on two meanings of *catch* (Act II, Sc. 3, 64-70); on two meanings of *time* (Act II, Sc. 3, 104-6); on two meanings of *pains* (Act II, Sc. 4, 67-8); on two uses of *O* (Act II, Sc. 5, 145-6); on two meanings of *by* (Act III, Sc. 1, 2-3).

Question 5.

Discuss the title of the play.

Answer

The first title of the play *Twelfth Night* would suggest to an Elizabethan audience a comedy in which a certain amount of joviality and frolic might be expected, and in which serious subjects, if treated at all, would be handled only with the lightest touch. The festival to which it refers took place on January 6th, and was characterized, much as Christmas Day is with us, by family gatherings and reunions at which games were played and fun was the order of the day. One of the customs associated with the festival was the election of kings and queens by use of beans and peas. A large cake, called Twelfth Cake and containing a bean and a pea, was divided up into sections, and the lady and gentleman who obtained respectively the pieces containing the pea and the bean were accepted as queen and king for the day. It is possible that this custom suggested to Shakespeare the name and character of his play in which fortune plays so large a part in the determining of the various husbands and wives.

The second title, *What You Will*, may be taken as indicating either (1) Shakespeare's indifference to the title, as though he meant to say, "here is a light comedy written for Twelfth Night, you may call it what you will," or (2) the difficulty of precisely cataloguing it, as though he said, "The play is neither pure comedy not romance, nor yet a masque, you may call it what you will."

Question 6.

How does the device of mistaken identity figure into the plot of *Twelfth Night*?

Answer

Mistaken identity was a favorite device used by comic dramatists throughout history. In *Twelfth Night*, the whole play is set into motion

110

by Viola's successful disguise as Cesario. Through her close contact with Orsino, as his servant, she is given the opportunity to fall in love with him; as a result of serving his requests, she comes into contact with Olivia and becomes the object of her love. Thus, the love triangle, which forms the central plot of the comedy is a direct result of mistaken identity.

When Sebastian finally arrives in Illyria, the romantic plot is first complicated even more, and then finally resolved. Viola can identify herself and win Orsino, and Olivia can finally marry the 'man' (at least the image of the man) she loves so deeply.

In the subplot, mistaken identity, again, first complicates matters, and then resolves them. If Viola had not been mistaken for a boy, then Olivia would not have fallen in love with her; if she had not fallen in love with Viola, then Sir Andrew would not have become jealous of her and challenged her to a duel. As a result of the duel, Antonio felt compelled to interfere, thinking that Viola was Sebastian, and was sent to prison. Further, when Sir Toby and Sir Andrew had mistaken Sebastian for Cesario, they ended up getting soundly beaten, and perhaps even learned a lesson from their experience. Not until Sebastian shows up, at the same time as Viola is present, do matters get cleared away.

Malvolio was also affected by mistaken identity, in two ways: first, if he had not been mistaken as to the identity of the author of the letter that led to his downfall, the whole conspiracy against him would have backfired; second, his mistaking Feste as the priest, Topas, is the source of considerable comedy in the play, and Feste's opportunity to enjoy a more personal revenge.

Question 7.

Discuss the use of contrast in *Twelfth Night* in (a) setting, and (b) character.

Answer

(a) The play contrasts the romantic setting of Illyria and Orsino's palace, with that of Olivia's self-chosen seclusion with the realistic and comic setting of her household, in which Sir Toby holds his revels and carries out his practical jokes at the expense of Malvolio and Sir Andrew. This contrast of romance and of comedy, moving on a lower plane, heightens the peculiarities of both.

(b) Different kinds of love are contrasted. Orsino is in love with love; Olivia loves passionately, overcoming her dignity and pride for the sake of a page; Viola loves without selfishness, serving the Duke's interests at the risk of harming her own. The comic characters love differently again; Maria is after Sir Toby's position and means, and likes his jovial nature; Malvolio is interested in authority and wealth, and feeds his vanity, imagining that Olivia loves him.

Sir Toby's sense of humor, his originality, loudness and courage are contrasted with Sir Andrew's stupidity, imitativeness, and cowardice.

Malvolio's gravity, sternness, and lack of humor are contrasted with the gaiety, easy living, and love of fun of Sir Toby, Feste, Fabian, and Maria. Maria's small size, sharp tongue, vivacity and impudence set off Olivia's noble beauty, dignity and formality.

Question 8.

It is noteworthy that both the comedy and the romance of the play meet together so naturally in Feste. Show how Feste's role in the play justifies this opinion.

Answer

Feste is a clown who combines in his make-up comic elements tinged with sentimental pathos in places. He provides a link between the moods of the main plot and the subplots.

He takes part in the merrymaking of Sir Toby and Sir Andrew and, in his role as clown, is himself the source of much comedy. He leads in the singing of catches, proving as boisterous as Sir Toby, himself. He torments Malvolio by his clowning in front of the cell. In his association with the schemers, we see him sharing in the lower, farcical comedy of the play.

Feste has a considerably greater share in the higher comedy of wit and sparkling repartee. He displays his peculiar logic before Maria, Olivia, Viola and the Duke, delighting them with his verbal skill and the freedom with which he tells them his opinions of them. His impersonation of Sir Topas is also proof of his subtler humor.

He is very fond of music, carrying his small drum around with him. He aids in heightening the sentiment of the main plot by the pathos of his lament "Come away, come away, death": his love-song "O mistress mine," though sung before Sir Toby and Sir Andrew, has reference to the main plot also, to the mutual pursuit and search for love of Orsino, Olivia and Viola. Feste's last song, "When that I was," sums up the spirit of the play, its mixture of comic sense and nonsense, of sentiment and pathos. The choice of songs sung by Feste is representative of these varied elements, and his part in the plotting of Sir Toby and Maria, his singing for Orsino, and his jesting with him, his mistress and Viola, shows him providing a focal point for the different moods of the play.

Question 9.

Show, with reference to specific situations and incidents, how the comic absurdities of Sir Toby and Sir Andrew are heightened by the use of contrast.

Answer

Sir Toby is robust, full of life, good humor, and inventiveness. Sir Andrew is weak and pale in appearance, passive, stupid and unoriginal. Sir Toby is responsible for practical jokes; Sir Andrew falls victim to his schemes.

Sir Toby is not offended by Maria's sharp tongue, he enjoys her scolding and teases her by praising Sir Andrew and by insisting on his right to drink. Sir Andrew is no match for Maria, who completely puts him down with little effort.

Sir Toby is energetic in his speech, showing a rough sense of humor in his puns, teasing, and use of odd words. Sir Andrew apes his manner, trying to make an impression on Maria; he repeats his words constantly, and picks up new terms from others like Viola. He has no original sense of humor.

Sir Toby thinks up schemes; he gaily makes Sir Andrew spend his money on him, and twice makes him send for more. He shuts Malvolio up in the cell. He arranges the farcical duel between Sir Andrew and Viola. He enjoys dominating Sir Andrew, punishing Malvolio for his self-conceit, and frightening the duelists with imaginary accounts of each other's valor. Sir Andrew is uninventive in deed as in word. He does not contribute anything to the action of the subplots, except that he is the victim. He is putty in Sir Toby's hands, falling for his promise that he will win Olivia, and easily pushed into the duel with Viola to gain Olivia's favor.

Sir Toby is blustering in his manner, believing in the strength of swearing. He is also courageous in accepting challenges. He takes his wound with nonchalance. Sir Andrew is boastful of his dancing, fencing and courage. He says that he hates "policy" and prefers fighting an enemy. He proposes a challenge to Malvolio without turning up for the duel. He is persuaded to fight Viola, writes a silly challenge, then tries to get out of the duel. He is willing to fight, if no bloodshed is allowed to take place. He runs after Viola when he hears her called a coward. He threatens to charge Sebastian with assault, for striking him, and moans over his wounds.

Question 10.

Describe the character of Orsino, and contrast it with that of Sebastian.

Answer

Orsino is described as "a noble duke in nature as in name." He is well reputed, "of great estate, of fresh and stainless youth," handsome, generous, "free, learned and valiant." With all these amiable and excellent qualities, however, he does not command our unqualified admiration. He is a man of self-indulgent love fancies, introspective, more concerned with the theme of love rather than love itself. Hence, unlike Sebastian, he cannot be said to be a forthright and sincere character. His advantages and undoubted accomplishments qualify him to inspire love in others, but his own love is not of the kind to be taken seriously. He is imaginative, possesses a soul for music and poetry, and expresses beautiful thoughts in exquisitely delicate and poetical language, but he has no strong convictions and shows himself inconsistent in word and deed.

Sebastian is the very antithesis of Orsino. He is, indeed, the complement of Viola, what she would have been had she been in reality what she professed to be (a boy). He is a man of action, fond of adventure, fresh and vigorous, modest and brave, no sentimentalist, but able to entertain a deep and abiding love. Unlike the Duke, Sebastian is a man of few words; his thoughts do not take the form of poetical imagery, yet we know that his feelings are deep-seated. We see him in the play as a loving brother, a warm and faithful friend, and we may be sure that "having sworn truth" he will become a true, sympathetic and helpful husband to Olivia.

Question 11.

What is meant by dramatic irony? Illustrate your explanation by reference to the play.

Answer

When a character on a stage speaks words which have a fuller significance for the audience than for the characters to whom the words are addressed we have an example of the device known as dramatic irony. Illustrations are numerous in those scenes in which Viola, in the disguise of a page, converses with the Duke or Olivia. In these scenes (cf. Act I, Sc. 4 and 5; Act II, Sc. 4; Act III, Sc. 1) expressions occur which would have more significance for the audience, knowing Viola to be a woman, than for the persons addressed. The following examples will make this clear:

> Duke.   What kind of woman is't?
>
> Viola.   Of your complexion.
>
> Duke.   She is not worth thee then. What years, i'faith?
>
> Viola.   About your years, my lord.
>
> Duke.   Too old by heaven.

Here, Viola's speeches would have more point for the audience than for the Duke, who would see in them only so much as Viola intended him to see.

In Act III, Scene 1, the following conversation takes place between Olivia and Viola:

> Olivia. I prithee, tell me what thou think'st of me.
>
> Viola. That you do think you are not what you are.
>
> Olivia. If I think so, I think the same of you.
>
> Viola. Then think you right; I am not what I am.

Here Olivia speaks more truth than she thinks she is speaking, and Viola speaks ambiguously without appearing to. The audience, at the same time, perceives the mystery and possesses the key to its interpretation.

Question 12.

Quote from the play allusions to Puritans. Do you suppose that we can infer Shakespeare's religious opinions from this play?

Answer

Sir Toby has made some inquiry about Malvolio, to which Maria answers:

> *Maria.*   Marry, sir, sometimes he is a kind of puritan.
>
> *Sir And.*   O! if I thought that, I'd beat him like a dog!
>
> *Sir To.*   What, for being a puritan? Thy exquisite reason, dear knight?
>
> *Sir And.*   I have no exquisite reason for 't, but I have reason good enough.
>
> *Maria.*   The devil a puritan that he is, or anything constantly, but a time-pleaser.

From this passage and from others even more ambiguous in other plays, Dr. Brandes has argued that from *Twelfth Night* onwards, Shakespeare has carried on "an unremitting war against Puritanism, conceived as hypocrisy." He tells us, moreover, that "it was a consequence of his position as an actor and theatrical manager that he saw only the ugliest side of Puritanism — the one it turned towards him."

This view, however, does not seem quite correct. Had Shakespeare intended to satirize the Puritans he would have made his intention clear and not have left it to Sir Andrew to express his dislike of them. Indeed, it would be small credit to any man or body of men to have gained the esteem or disdain of such a numbskull as Sir Andrew. Further, it seems quite as likely that the poet intended the satire to be directed against the knight's unreasoning hostility against a body of men, famous chiefly for their efforts in the direction of freedom of thought and religion, as that he is expressing his own animosity against a meek and long-suffering people. The fact is, that Shakespeare lived in an age of political and religious heat, yet there is in his words no sectarian character of politics or religion. "The spirit of his faith is not to be ascertained by bringing together little sentences from the utterances of this one of his *dramatis personae*, and of that. By such a method he might be proved an atheist."

Bibliography

Barnet, Sylvan. "Charles Lamb and the Tragic Malvolio,"
Philological Quarterly, XXXIII (1954).

Biswas, Dinesh. *Shakespeare's Treatment of His Sources
in the Comedies*. Philadelphia, 1977.

Downer, Alan S. "Feste's Night," *College English*, XIII (1952).

Draper, John W. *The Twelfth Night of Shakespeare's Audience*.
New York, 1972.

Goldsmith, Robert H. *Wise Fools in Shakespeare*.
East Lansing, Mich., 1955.

Hollander, John. "*Twelfth Night* and the Morality of Indulgence,"
Sewanee Review, LXVII (1959).

Hotson, Leslie. *The First Night of Twelfth Night*. New York, 1954.

Jenkins, Harold. "Shakespeare's *Twelfth Night*," *Rice Institute
Pamphlets*, XLV (1959).

King, Walter N., ed. *Twentieth Century Interpretations of
"Twelfth Night."* Englewood Cliffs, N.J., 1968.

Knight, G. Wilson. *The Shakespearian Tempest*.
London, 1932, 1953.

Leech, Clifford. *"Twelfth Night" and Shakespearian Comedy*.
Toronto, 1965.

Lewalski, Barbara K. "Thematic Patterns in *Twelfth Night*,"
ShakS 1 (1965).

Mueschke, Paul, and Jeannette Fleisher. "Jonsonian Elements in the
Comic Underplot of *Twelfth Night*," *PMLA*, XLVIII (1933).

Salingar, L.D. "The Design of *Twelfth Night*," *SQ*, IX (1958).

Seiden, Melvin. "Malvolio Reconsidered," *University of
Kansas City Review*, XXVIII (1961).

Tilley, Morris P. "The Organic Unity of *Twelfth Night*,"
PMLA, XXIX (1914).

Welsford, Enid. *The Fool*. London, 1935.

Williams, Porter, Jr. "Mistakes in *Twelfth Night*
and Their Resolution," *PMLA*, LXXVI (1961).